MW00583113

Concert
At The White House

Norm Gubber
Tulalip, Washington, USA

ISBN 978-0-6151-8820-1
Printed In the United States of America.

This is a work of fiction. Any character resemblance to
real persons, living or dead, is of pure coincidence.

Other writings:

It's Where You Find It (2006)
Laura's Letters (2007)

Thanks for your continued encouragement and assistance—

All friends and relatives who know me beyond "hello". You all listen, and I learn. What would my world be without you?

CHAP 1. Presidential material

Dad understood. Ray retold the details to us, about how he did it, right after he got out of the hospital. Not hurt except for dehydration and sunburn. He'd tell the story a couple times later as we grew older. Finally grew out of the story. Me, I remember it like yesterday.

At first he was gonna hide in the rocks nearby, but then thought about exposure and sunburn and all that he got anyway. He said after thinking about it, he made a wickie hut of some sort, a wickiup some call it, like the Diggers used to do. Then he just waited.

Waiting is a challenge for everyone. The ones he's after is real good at it too. Two jugs of water and a few bags of California mix. No cooking of any kind. He didn't want to leave a scent. Them wild ones is real keen on scenting. They got pretty good eyesight too, but in the end, it's the smell that keeps 'em out of trouble. Yep, it was the smell o' him he blamed it on. He thought the horses might've smelled the peanuts or something in the trail mix. That's what he blamed himself later for it taking so long.

And then he waited more. He had a plan to herd them against the sharp edges of the carved mountain. While he waited, he thought about how he and Dad and me went there a couple weeks before to build the V-shaped corral at the edge of the desert in a mountain arroyo. Got into his thoughts a lot. Played it back mentally. Nothing else to do for now.

Most people can stand the first day by themselves, but by the second, thinking about it gets old. I never want to be a prisoner in solitary. Nothing to do in cramped quarters. Can't move in or out. Where he was he never could tell when the herd might show up. First sign someone's about and they don't come back for months. Find new watering elsewhere.

He continued to wait. When he woke up at times in the night and early mornings, he stretched himself to take out the kinks, then swiped a handful of mix and a sip of water. He knew how to ration water without getting dehydrated. We had a lot of practice as kids growing up.

Daytime he peeked between twigs constructed of sage and some willow boughs brought from near home, talking to his thoughts all the time. Like how he parked his pickup couple miles away and hauled the stuff in.

You gotta understand about Ray. He ain't exactly people lovin' like ma and me. Lot like dad. He can stand to be around people, all right, but he can stand to be alone by himself too. That's how dad and him figured he could do it. Dad told him to plan for at least a week. No sign, he could signal. We'd come help him out. Try some other time.

Then nothing. He knew they came here where they dug in dirt for trickles of water in springtime. Every day, for a week at a time, he had spotted them from the same position me and dad was gonna watch for him now. Wait for the signal to come in.

And he waited. Two days went by. Down half of the mix. Then he checked his eating. With nothing to do but think and eat, he realized he might have to make it last. He could've left but he stuck it out. Told my dad not to come for him till he signaled. That's the way Ray operated. Set his mind and followed through. Not his approach to the presidency, but that was the only exception.

Three days, four, five, he waited. By now he was so hungry, he almost didn't care. Last drop of water fresh out. One more day, he thought to himself, as he told us later on. Course, as the story gets told over the years, he embellishes a little, like saying he was ready to stay another week if he had to.

On the sixth day they came. A big mottled gray pawed the ground like he knew something was up, the urge to drink getting the best of him. A lead mare took them in, past Ray's wickie without detecting odor. Paid no attention to the reconstruction of the corral. Been coming here before without incident. Smarter ones might've smelled the new wood pieces of log fencing.

When several more got past him, Ray decided to make his move. He got up and crawled out without them noticing. But he had forgot to stretch. When he got up and out on twos, he went down on all fours. The last of the herd went back; the others toward the V-corral forward of the crag. Ray hobbled, tripped, then forgot his pain and ran, waving his arms, closing the gate behind two. Three others ran up the outsides, turned quick-like and ran back past him to join the free ones, where the stallion seemed to be calling them back, according to Ray. But Ray had two.

Dad and me waited across the valley on another jut of rocks, daily, near the end of the day, for two days straight; then another two, same way, at the spotting position. We took turns scoping Ray. Could just barely make out the wickie. No movement. Couple times, I wanted to go in and see if he was okay. Dad said no.

"He's fine," he said.

There it was, to my relief. It came back to us on that sixth day, before we got the scope ready. A mirror flash from below the notch. Ray had climbed one side of the mountain above the pen and flashed us like we planned. After we hurried to set up the scope, we could see the pen with two horses trapped. He'd done it!

We returned a flash, and dad yelled, "Let's go." It was gonna take us almost an hour just to get there over sand and cutting rock. Lose a tire fast out here if you hit those sharp rocks just right.

"Water?" Dad asked me.

"Yep. Five-gallon jug. Remembered," I answered.

When we got to him, he had a rope halter on one of them and the other kept circling the inside looking for an escape route. Ray was a mess. He looked weak and tired from sitting all day. He was part sunburned and had a little trouble walking. Dad insisted on taking him by the clinic hospital on the way back. Ray protested, but in the end, knew dad was right. Told us about it while some tubes trickled liquid in his arm. Had to have some festering cactus thorns removed too. But he was used to that.

Says he went out only at night to dig a trench and use a toilet. Dug everything deep and buried it. He had sunburn welts on his back, neck and arms where he had been sitting next to the twigs for hours, the sun coming through, making zebra-stripe hatches on his skin. Minimum clothing. Shorts only. Wanted his smell to blend with the surroundings.

Thought it all out in advance. No sweating. Only one night of storm. That was bath night. Only two nights of bowel movement, two pockets in the desert, tamped down waiting for dung beetles; then his colon shut down. But he had his mustang and one for me if I wanted it. I did.

Why didn't he give up? You had to know Ray. He never gave up on anything he put his mind to. That's what we all admired about Ray. Let me say about his stubbornness.

On the track team in high school. Told the coach he was a dash man. Coach looked him over; coach raised his eyebrows. Ray's tall, on the gangly side. Not a dash man said the coach. Dash man said Ray.

His goal? To be third fastest in the school history. Practiced all the time. Dead last at the county meet when he was a freshman. Near to last as a sophomore. And so on. Finished his senior year; come in second on a state meet in Reno. Coach shook my dad's hand; wondered what we fed 'im.

Ray was in the hospital overnight with tubes stuck in to him and sunburn stuff on him. Greased up with antibiotic ointment after removing the needles. He never was sick, he told them. Dad wasn't taking no chances this time, he said; mom chastising him all the while for letting him do it.

Before bringing Ray back, and the one horse he managed to lasso, we tied the other to tires in the pen and let it drag 'em around for a while so he'd know who was boss. Put in a water tub to drink, then loaded the first on a horse trailer, brought up from the T-bone intersection where we left it. When we went back to get the one left behind, we figured it never did drink from the bucket. There was a bunch of holes dug inside and some wet sand at the bottom of most. A bloody chestnut. I liked mine better than Ray's, a small gray that looked like his paw that came in first time Ray spotted them, so he told us.

We trained 'em and rode 'em for years, even after Ray graduated college and we moved up near to Wild Horse. Cheap horseflesh dad would say, when we scuzzed beer and talked about the time Ray trapped some wild mustangs at the edge of the Black Rock.

Chap 2. I'm the president's brother, and I approve the following:

We're invited to the White House for the first time this coming weekend since my brother got elected three years ago. He's trying to make up for that bad playing he did at his inauguration. Big crowd and everyone noisy is what he mostly blamed it on. He's right too. Not amplified, you know. Shoulda known better.

Besides, with all that time spent hob-knobbin' and carousing, he didn't have any time to practice, right? No wonder he looked like a fool. Should've stayed with speech-makin'; what he's good at. He can charm the button right off a blouse, if you know what I mean. Think he has too.

This time he took some lessons from a

guy in Los Angeles. His name escapes me . . .
something like Parkinson . . . or, "Lula! What's
that guys name that gave Ray those lessons in
the White House?" Damn, I forget. She's told
me not to yell at her. Wants me to come right
up in her face and talk sensibly if I got a question or want to say something to her.

Lula? Lula Anne—that's my wife's name.
From the South, so they give her two names,
right? That's my better half I'm calling at. She
remembers the names of everyone. I'm good
with faces. Her with names. We're quite a team,
right?

"Lula! You there?"

Now I gotta yell, cause I don't know
where she's at. Honestly, I don't know what that
woman does all day. She's a good cook though,
and always has fixin's ready on time. On time
when I wanna eat, that is. Recent years though,
we eat and sleep most any time. Ain't like when
we was both working. Like if she's got a story
to finish writing or is in the middle of a book
she's reading. She might tell me to fix a peanut
butter and jelly while I'm waiting. Once in a
while, I cook too. But she's so much better at it.

"You calling me, Ed?" she yells back.
Ah, there she is.

"What was that guy's name, you know,
the one that gave Ray some guitar lessons?"

"Parkinson. Christopher Parkinson. No . .
. Chris . . . not Parkinson. Parkinson's that dis-
ease. He's not a disease. Real good guitarist.
Something like that though," she yells back.

"Why?"

We're always talking at long distance even if we don't want to. Both have strong voices as a result. You want to know what's going on in this house, you don't need an amplifier. If a window's open, you can hear us ten miles down the street.

Ed Ransom said the other day, "Ed, I didn't know you bought a new mower." He's another Ed; lives two houses away. Sometimes when we're a yellin' back and forth, he'll answer Lula. Makes her real mad.

I said, "How'd you know it so soon? Just got it this a.m."

He said, "I heard you telling Smith next door 'bout it."

He's right. I remember opening the bedroom window upstairs when I saw my neighbor, Smith, walkin' around my new mower parked on my side of the hedges. "How you like my new mower?" I yell to him.

"Got a new one, I see," he calls back.

"Yep, 14 horses."

"Gonna do my yard too?"

"Like hell. Buy yourself one. They're on sale at Wal-Mart. Better hurry, going fast."

I do most of my shopping at Wal-Mart. Why not? I know, I know. They've got sweatshops around the world that feed in low wage stuff to 'em. But I'm on a fixed income now. Gotta do like the rest of us. 'Sides, ain't that what that NAFTA, or something like it is all about? Only extended to include the rest of the

world? Let the Chinese make it and keep all
that industrial pollution over there. Let them get
blamed for global warming for a change. In the
meantime, my problems extend only to my
neighborhood. And Smitty.

Smitty tries to keep that lawn mower of
his going. Takes him ten minutes to get it
started anymore. It's a Snapper, he brags. I don't
care what it is. When it finally outlives its use-
fulness, get a new one. No way I'd spend ten
minutes trying to get a mower started. Two
pulls or else. Fair warning to all you lawnmow-
ers out there. If you don't wanna make the scrap
heap, start within two pulls. Then you gotta
keep at it; fixin' things on it, I'm talkin' about.

Just the other day I told him about his
grass looking uneven. He said his shields, or
something like that, was worn away to a fraz-
zle, and bent so bad his blades crooked at an
angle. "Still cuts though," he says, "I sharpen
the blades every other time."

He might as well sharpen throwing
knives and try to cut his grass that way. "Smith,
you need a new mower," I says to him at the
end of his day that took about twice as long as
mine.

We got the same size lawns. Planted
them at the same time when we moved here a
few years ago. Rented the same roller and took
turns helping roll the seed on. He helped me
with my sprinkler system and I helped with his.
His came up faster. Mine grew thicker when it
filled in.

"Can't afford another Snapper," he says. "Have you checked the prices lately?"

You'd think we had an all-day field to mow. He shoulda been back with us on the ranch when we was trying to grow hay. Get just enough for the two horses. When we got a coupla steer, had to import some hay from California. Haul it in and feed it to the cattle. Horses just eat up your profits. It's the fun part of ranchin' life. All I got is about a half-acre to mow. Takes me about two hours to do mine. Ten or fifteen mows over the summer with Saint Augustine. Change the oil every spring. That's about it. The cheapest one at Wal-Mart'll do that.

Can't convince Ed though. Needs a Snapper. Thumbs his nose at a Murray. I tell him they're made up there in Tennessee. Them country folk up there know what they're doing. He agrees, but gotta have a Snapper. Buy second-hand? Nope, not for him. New or nothing.

Saw a Snapper in the Nickel ads the other day. Two years old. When I cut it out and give it to him, he puts it on his bench and says he might look into it. I know what that means. He's waiting for me to disappear around my garden shed, and into the trash it goes. Next time I ask if he looked into it, he stares and says he don't remember my giving it to him. Lotsa games with absentee players going on 'round here. We talk sometimes with missing parts too.

"How's he doing?" Smith says. Course, I know who he's talkin' about, but I pretend I don't.

"Just fine," I say. "Think he'll be out of the hospital soon. Took half his stomach and some of his intestines."

"Huh?" he says, "Guess I've been missing the news."

"Oh yeah?" I say. "Not only that, but his wife's pregnant again."

"Huh? Oh, I know what you're doing. Your brother," he centralizes, "the President."

"Oh," I say, "thought you were talking about Will Jeffries."

"Why did you think that? I never even brought it up."

"You didn't? Hmmm, must be getting senile," I say. I then go into the old routine of the three things that happen to a person when they get old. Course, he finishes the joke before I get started and we get back to nonsense talk all over again.

We come from different places, Smith and me. He was brought up in New England and me in Nevada. Heck it was two weeks after I met him that I even knew where New England was. Not strong on geography in the West schools. I thought it was someplace overseas, like maybe they reinvented England or something.

Now here we are, both of us in Florida. Made sense for him, but everyone keeps askin' why I'm here. Not natural for someone from the West to retire in the East. Supposed to go to Arizona or somewhere. Maybe California. How about Southern Nevada, like Laughlin? Hear they're filling up the place.

The water, I answer, and something that happened to me when I was back home, young and frivolous. Tell you about it later. Course I'm remembering what happened to Ray and the wild horses he trapped for us. Learned a lot about the importance of water in that week.

The water?

Yep. They ain't none out there anymore. Even have to ask for it when you go to a restaurant. In Florida, you got all you want. Go to Georgia. The same. Go to the Carolinas. Same. To Kentucky—well in Kentucky, it depends where you go. If you go east, the water might be as bad as some places out West. The West is running out fast, and what's left ain't worth drinking. Maybe for the Northwest, where they still seem to have a good amount of it. But with luck, they'll ruin it too. Casinos use a lot. Get my drift?

Buy bottled stuff you say? Not me. Damn if I'll pay more for water that I do for my gas. Move where it is. When they ruin it there, move on. Without water, life ain't worth living anywhere. And if we don't take care of this global warming problem real soon, we're gonna find out more'n we want to about how to save our water.

Ray knows it and is working on it. Chances are he won't have enough time in eight years, that is, if he decides to run again, like I don't think he will.

His wife's more cut out for the office than him. She could be the first woman president, the way she goes. Has about half the country on her side right now, but I'll tell you more about that later on too.

Lookit them Israelis. You might think they're fighting over all that land, but what they're really fighting over is water. And when it gets too expensive to make, all that fighting is gonna stop and they're gonna move on. Maybe to the mountains of Italy or somewhere. Maybe to Florida. Hell, here it just runs out of the ground naturally. Springs all over the place. They even name towns after 'em. Gallons and gallons per minute. All turns to salt just a few miles away. A few miles by Nevada standards, that is.

So, I ain't so dumb as my neighbors think. Picked my place to retire. Course it helped that Lula Anne was from here. Course too, being the president's kin, soon as they find out, makes me ten times as smart as I really am. Some people think it makes me dumber though. From the other parties. Did I forget to mention that Ray got elected as the first Independent? More about that later if I'm inclined to remember.

My brother's smart about a lot of things, like global warming, but he's pretty dumb about other stuff, about water. Hell, he grew up out West, same as me. Think he'd know better. Now wants to open all that land where we come from for private investment. Has become the mouthpiece for the BL and M. Those politicians got him turned around on that issue. Can't wait to tell him what I think about it. Don't have him, or his thinking figured out right now. He was always against them main critters when we grew up and Dad taught us who to be weary of. Hell, all they ever done was to support the mining interests and development and continue to ruin the state. We can blame that on the same mentality that's always wrecked the state. Here's the way I see it.

They're all from the East with no water problems. Make big enough salaries to drink bottled water besides. Won't clean up their reservoirs and make it practical to drink from the tap either. Don't know where they get off anymore. Not on the subway I ride anyhow.

So, if Ray decides to sign the bill, we got another land stampede like they did in the olden days. They'll start tearing down those rancher's fences in no time. Course you know them ranchers been squatting on public land for years. Bring back the six-shooters. It'll take 'em about a year to turn the whole place into another dust bowl. Hell, it already is becoming that with all the surface mining and all.

I just can't figure it. All the water that is around for every man, woman and child, and somehow we failed to protect it. Who ever thought we'd be paying on the nose for clean water to drink? Not the Pilgrims, I bet. And now I hear on the news a couple days ago that about half of the bottled stuff may be unsafe to drink. Hell, if I had a well and the inclination, I'd probably be selling the stuff too.

Pollution. That's another problem. Never mind the sulfur, the nitrates, the arsenic, and the pesticides that are gettin' in it down here in Florida, too. Most of the cost is making the plastic anyway. Take away the plastic and you could sell it for a penny a glass and still make a thousand percent profit. Course, it'd be inconvenient to sell it by the glass.

Where's all that plastic ending up anyhow? That's why they got a big mound in a lot of counties down here. No mountains in Florida? Just wait and see. They cover them with something they can plant grass over, put in drainage ramps and the like. But it's still garbage. Mostly plastic, I bet.

CHAP 3. The president's wife

Martha, the president's wife, is my sister-in-law. She's always hated her name. Started spelling it different when she was a freshman in high school. This is all stuff we've learned about her over the years. She don't mind telling it to anyone. Sometimes Ray has her to *hush her mouth*, as they say down here in Florida.

Joined the cheerleading team. Skinny like a stick figure. No boobs at all. She did like the others—stuffed her training bras with toilet paper. Boobs were important then. Not like today where those gals parade the ramps in clothes a hundred yards too big for 'em, and try to walk crooked. None of them eat more than a hundred calories a day from what I hear. Walking skeletons. Kids (me too) like to look at 'em, but I don't think they copy them much.

Look around. Kids everywhere, specially a lot of young girls are as fat as ever. Don't get the idea; two hands on the edge of the table and PUSH! All this diet stuff, and they still gain weight. Good for the diet books and companies. Fat in the wallet. Know what I mean?

Anyway, Martha Galway, used to be Martha Maples, started writing her name as M-A-A-R-T-H-A, about half way through her freshman year. Everyone on the cheerleading squad *oooed* and *aaaahed* over it at first. "Soo gennteeel!" Suzie Framingham gushed over her in the locker room.

"I juust loove iit," drawled Rita Cummings. You gotta understand how them Southern gals talk. If it's a one-syllable word, they make two or more of it. Just the opposite if it's more'n one.

Martha accepted the flattery and began heading all her papers as *Maartha*. Miss Evans, I guess I should call her *Ms.* Evans now, took exception.

"Forget how to spell your name?" she returned a paper with a C- minus at Martha's desk. Martha can't answer. The C-minus brought more attention than she wanted right then.

"Could I talk with you later?" Martha whispers to Ms. Evans walking along the aisle.

"I've decided to change my first name," Martha tells her teacher.

"What's wrong with the one you were given?"

"That's it, Miss Evans. It's so . . . plain. And you're right, ma'am. It was given to me. I think people should be able to choose their names when they get old enough, don't you?"

Many, many points made with Abigail Evans. Both her folks is teachers. Like she didn't have no choice herself. Called sympathizing, or something like that. I'll have to ask Lula.

"Just keep it consistent," Ms. Evans dismisses her.

Martha ends up freshman English with a C-minus average. Her teacher, Ms. Evans, gives her another grade at the bottom of the report card in the comment section: "A-plus in social skills!"

Martha's still getting a *A-plus*. Especially when she's trying to attack what she calls *social* problems. To hear her tell it on TV, that's the problem with all this war talk, the budget, urban housing, saving the environment, education and crime: people lack social skills. *"Can't we all get along?"* is her favorite sayin'. Course, I think it's borrowed from somewhere.

And what is her solution to these many problems? More game playing and exercise at the national, even the international level. Yep, I can see it now—all you kids in Ethiopia–line up for thirty minutes of pushups this morning. Sorry if you haven't ate in three days, that's not my problem—exercise is. And it'll be your salvation too. Got to get the energy flowing to the brain. Not that you've got any left, with all that protein missing in your formative years. I just got through reading an article about that. Now just follow along with First Lady Maartha, and a-one, a-two; and a-one, a-two . . . in Lawrence Welk tempo.

Hell, she's got another video coming out this month. *Be First, with the First Lady*–it's gonna be called. Some of this bothers Ray, but he don't let on much. I read him though; always have.

When Ray sent us an invitation to the White house, he phoned a few days afterward and told me. "Don't tell her I said anything about it," he cautioned. Just like always, the right hand don't know what the left hand is do-ing in his own house. The White House at that.

He ogles on the side, but as far as I know, don't touch. Probably learned his lesson from that Clinton guy. Besides, he's no hugger and I suppose it's got to start somehow. Feel 'em first, and if you like it–go for it. Ha. My wife hates it when I say that. Just a habit. Like that saying about the four F's.

"Buddy," she says, "if a good looking woman was to come along and tickle your pecker, you'd just flush like a quail and try to remember it long enough till the next time you jump on me. Isn't that right hon?"

I'm thinkin', where'd she come up with this *Buddy* name. I guess she's right at that. Never did find a better-looking woman than her. Everything natural. Still in its place at our age. Forget about fixin' anything that's natural.

Not like Martha. Before she got out of high school, started taking some hormones, or whatever those pills are the guys pass around the locker room to build muscles. She had so much energy, that when she became head cheerleader, half the girls almost quit. She'd keep them an extra hour or two after the regular practice routines; humpin' and pumpin' till some fell on their backs, out cold. Even an ambulance came once to take one of the girls to the hospital emergency room. Total dehydration, the doctor on call said.

Mothers started to call her folks and say that Martha was a tyrant, and they wouldn't blame their daughters if they all quit the team.

When Martha started to grow some extra hair around her upper lip and on one boob, according to my wife, she began to slow down on the pills. By then her boobs had grown big enough anyway. Mostly muscle from under the fat. When she finally did slow down, her size went down two inches with it. That's when she began to give serious thought to a boob job. Her folks begin to feed into that though.

"Not with my money and insurance," her pa told her. "You can do it after you get married, on your own terms," her father says.

When she took cosmetology in junior college, the ladies there begin to teach her how to construct everything favorable to the attraction of men. She learned fast. Having natural boobs was no problem. You keep just enough

flesh showing at all times. Before long, imagi-
nation makes them a lot bigger than they really
are. Short-waisted? Wear clothes with long
lines to show off your better assets; like your
legs. Bow-legged? Synthetic pants that covered
the gap as you walk. Braces on your teeth? Yes,
even at this age. One year can make a lot of difference. And cover those jutting ears with hair,
lady. Watch and listen to the customers who
come in here with all their airs and conversation
about wealth. Then emulate them.

It worked. Before she'd finished her first
year, she was singing like Tammy Wynette and
looking like Dolly Parton. Ray saw her at a
dance at an amusement park and fell in love in-
stantly. Presidents is easy to fool with girl kinda
stuff. Read up on 'em, you'll find out.

CHAP 4. More about Ray

We might be getting ready to go to war again. Ray's been up late nights mulling over the new Iran crisis. Some diplomats got assassinated in Tehran and that got the United Nations started. Our new ambassador wants to right every wrong that ever existed and her brother is an advisor at the National Security Council. So naturally, that gets the ball rolling and here we go again. No sooner do we get out of the Desert Storm situation, the second Desert Storm, the Bosnia deal and the Kosovo crisis, and here we go again. Still ain't done with the new Iraq thing. Guys getting torn up over there, coming home with enough brains to make a fruit salad. Jeeze, ain't we ever gonna learn to stop trying to solve the world's problems?

Why all this happens is beyond me, but I shouldn't have too much to say about it I guess while living here in sunny Florida on a pension that comes in regular-like. But you gotta sit back and think about it once in a while ain't you? I mean, it's all over the news all the time, so how you gonna avoid it?

I've finally decided that we've inherited it all. Been reading the science and health section of some new weekly magazine my wife gave me as part of my birthday present. It's short, and encapsulates everything that's happened in the past week. That is if the post office gets it here on time. My wife'll like that *in-a-capsule* word.

Forgot to mention about her. She's a word freak. Likes to get me in those word games and all. Does the crosswords, the cryptic things and so on. Me, I just use enough to get by. But some's been slopping over. You'll probably figure all this out as I keep writing. But more about what I think of wars.

Not only that, but we seem to like to perpetuate it. Mostly religious wars. Starts with the Bible and it's lasting till today. Lookit the Old Testament. No sooner is the flood over, and Noah's three sons born, than war starts among the three tribes. Not only that, but prejudice starts with Ham and his kin too. Just because he sees the old man nekkid if I got my facts right. Sometimes I mix up all that Bible stuff. Anyways, one brother gets a little more than the other, or becomes jealous because someone is surviving with a better standard of living than the other, and a fight results. All this spills into the future of mankind too.

I remember hearing Clinton on TV once, about how he's fed-up with the persecutions in Palestine, Northern Ireland, ethnic cleansing in the Balkans, the caste system in India and he goes on and on, saying it's all silly. At the same time he's ordered us to bomb the Slavs. Teamwork with NATO he says. Teamwork all right. Our planes, our bombs, our men, our money. Teamwork, right. Yeah, even hit targets in Belgrade—no matter what the collateral damage is. That's a fancy way of saying it's too damn bad if a few civilians get in the way. I even heard my brother Ray adopting the same language the other day on TV. Damn, this stuff catches on fast. Almost not worth us coming here in the first place.

You know, when this country was invented, we all had a chance to bring something new here. Get rid of all that stuff about fighting our brothers and leave it back there in Europe where they seem to enjoy doing all that stuff. But no, the first thing we do is quote from Exodus, and begin to burn witches in Salem. Ray says we didn't burn any, just hung 'em. No matter, they're all dead anyhow.

The Mormons had it right. Invent a new Jesus in New York and start fresh in this country. But they couldn't avoid the old hang-ups either and started killing among themselves and harboring prejudice against others that weren't Mormon. I don't know. Sometimes I just want to give it all up. No wonder I don't go to church much no more.

Our religion wasn't too tight in Nevada. I don't know what Daddy was, but once in a while he'd go to the Catholic Church in Paradise Valley. Mostly he was busy on the farm Sundays. When he wasn't working for himself he was renting his labor to a fellow rancher. Hard to make it alone out West, unless you got a couple sections of land, which we didn't have. When my momma started driving, she'd take us to church in Winnemucca. It was fun to go there and then to the Basque's for a good feed. Had good Basques in Elko too. Miss that Basque food. Not any here in Florida I don't think.

Church and school, that's what mainly took up all our time. Me and Ray, that is. The folks had their own agenda. Course chores overlapped on us all.

Remember when pa got a new spread up near Wild Horse. Me and Ray went to a one-room. When I outgrew it, had to commute to Elko for high school. Ray stayed behind with our schoolteacher and the rest of the kids, that weren't many. Can you believe it? The president of the United States attended school in a one-room. Guess maybe Lincoln done it first. Things just seemed to be getting good. Getting even with the finances and all.

After pa got killed, still too painful to tell

all right now, momma sold out and put the money in investments for our future. I needed more than Ray I guess. He kept going on in school, getting all kinds of scholarships.

Me, I went to Reno, to the university for a couple years, and then dropped out after that. I just couldn't do all that studying. Probably got a year's worth in all. Besides, by then I was more interested in cars and my new job at the college in the music department. Did it for the rest of my life. Not at the college except for sometimes when they needed special work. Tuned pianos. Never was any good as a musician. But Ray was. Good at most things, he was.

Ray, he was into everything, just like he is now. Started with the cello, and then when the guitar got real popular in the sixties and seventies, he switched over. He's pretty good at it too, but no ace. About a king or a queen. Better'n a jack. He was just into so much stuff that he never had enough time to develop all the technical skills.

"I could be really good, if I had eight hours a day to practice," he'd say.

But he never took the eight. Not five, not three, sometimes two. But he learned a few classical pieces, good enough so that when he plays, he knows how to cover some things his fingers won't do.

So this coming Sunday night, about a week away, when we're at the White House, I'll be interested to see what new stuff this Parkin-

son fellow taught him. Still don't think I got
that name right so I'll ask again.

My wife just told me that the guy's name
is Parkening. See, I knew she'd get it right after
a while. She's good with names. I've got a picture of him in my head on the cover of an
album we got tucked away somewhere. That's
probably where she remembered the name.
Went to the album and found it. Ray bought it
for us back in the late seventies when he was
trying to practice more. That's when he gave a
concert at the local library while running for
state senator. He wasn't too bad, either. Got a
idea about that too.

How am I a music critic? You tune pianos for thirty years, and you see and hear a lot
of good players. After a while you begin to notice the difference among 'em. I ain't never
studied no instrument like Ray has. Oh, I
played the tuba in the marching band. But
blowing one note at a time's a lot different from
five or ten like them piano people do. And guitar players about half that much. More'n one
anyways.

The news is on so I guess I'll tune in to
see what my brother is saying about the situation now.

CHAP 5. Me, Ed Galway. More about my home life

My wife just came into the garage while I was trying to fit a back check on the rail of a piano action. Yes, I still do a lot of piano tuning and some repairs on the side. Getting near to lunchtime and she's probably wanting to know if I'm hungry. Sometimes she does a pun for lunch.

"Tuner?" she says. Course, she means "tuna".

By golly, by now she's learned how to say stuff to me properly. Used to be I would get a ten-line discourse. Hey, I like that word— don't know where it came from. On the kind of bread I wanted my sandwich on. Kind of mayonnaise? Toasted? Paper plate? Pickle on the side? Here or at the table? Now she's finally learned to say it right. I don't give a rat's ass about how I get it and she knows it. Long's it's fresh, including the bread, and not too much mayonnaise.

"Yep, I'll taker a *tuner* sandwich," I say back, emphasizing the word. Like the Yankees up north say. Like my neighbor, the other Ed. It's a little joke we started long time ago. Comes in regular-like now.

She'll bring it and just put it on the workbench and go back to her reading. Must be a nice life with nothing to do but read all day. I should talk. Mine ain't so bad either. But it's more than that; I should recognize it. Did I mention, she's also wrote a lot of kid's books lately? Mostly about how teenagers develop and such. She feels it's a important thing for them to know. "Mostly directed to kids at the middle school level," she says. Knows about it.

Used to be a teacher, she was. Retired, the same time I did, with a pretty good pension. Course her book royalties don't hurt us either. Sells a lot to schools all over the country. Well, her publisher does, that is.

Now we can sit back in our Florida room and relax all day if we want. Except for Tuesdays and Fridays when she wants to drag me over to the senior center to play bridge. I don't know shit about the game. Let me give you a typical scenario.

Someone asks if I open with a short club,

I say, "Okay." I know what it is, but I don't *really* know what it means. Two opponents'll start jabbering about things like: cue bids; Standard American Yellow Card; Michaels cue bid; weak twos and the like, before we get started. Then my partner opens. I bid three no trump—that's my favorite bid—and all that opponent talk is gone to waste. Except when I go set of course. That's about fifty percent of the time. Then the opponents got to ride me about taking their bid away. What a waste of goddam time and talk. But she likes to play, so it's one of the things we do together. Sometimes I manage to weasel out. I'm always looking for an excuse.

That's when I try to schedule a piano job or two. "I'll meet you there if I get done on time," I say. Mostly, I show up late, and they've already got enough players. I go home and for once I can watch the end of a basketball game, or some other jock stuff on TV. And then there's chores, most of which I don't mind doin'. That is, till I get pooped. She's usually got questions then.

She knows when I'm just about done and ready to come in for my afternoon nap. When I walk through the door, she's a-waitin'.

"What am I supposed to wear on Saturday?" she asks.

Now she asks. We've known about the gala before Ray's performance since two months. She hates to shop. Thinks she can still wear the same stuff she taught school in, and still does.

"You mean you ain't gone shopping yet?" I say.

"Oh, you know me. Hate to buy. Wear too. Maybe they'll accept me in these?" she says.

I look over, up and down; she looks like she did when I met her. She's got those yellow shorts on with the plain white T-shirt over it. The outline of her bra is struggling to hold up her large breasts. In recent years it's a tougher job. Her hair is short now, not like she used to keep it, long and flowing. Almost silver now. She refuses to color it. I can still remember the sheen it had.

And manners. Remember when we went out to supper once. She reached for the rest of the bread at the Basque's in Minden one night when me and mom was there.

"I touched it first," I said, knowing full well I was going to give in. Mom kinda dirty-looks me.

"Oh, sorry," she says, more apologetic than she had to be. "Just kidding, go 'head," I says.

"No, really. I've had enough already," she says. And it went from there to here, I guess. Must have got here somehow.

"Why don't you go with me?" she adds.

"What do I know about dresses? Why don't you call Maa-aa-rr-tha?"

"Sure. Like I need her advice on something to wear," she gives me one of those irritated looks. Course I know why. Never has got along with my sister-in-law. Thinks she's a phony right from the git-go. Course, is what she is too. But now she's got all that help in the White House to help her pick out the right stuff to wear. Probably has a dressing room attached somewhere, with a full taxpayer staff to help her pick out and fit into things.

Whenever I see her on TV she's always wearing something to show off her fake boobs and muscle arms. Ha, it was funny one day when she did a guest appearance live with some kids at Daytona during spring break. She was trying to show them how to keep fit and demonstrated a few steps from her exercise video. Right in the middle of a routine, one of the pads in her bra, yep that's right, she wears pads besides the boob job, well, it begin to slip, and she didn't notice. At the end, about half of it was out of the bra, and someone on the side motioned to cut and they switched to a commercial. When they returned she was back intact again and acted like nothing happened. But the news programs all made a to-do about it that night on the news.

I remember that Jennings guy reporting about it: "An interesting addition to Spring break occurred this afternoon with the First Lady's appearance as a guest at the annual Daytona Beach celebration . . . " This time it showed her quickly stuffing the pad back in, then the cameras panned several other young gals whose assets didn't need the extra padding.

Sometime between my nap and the evening news the back door opens and I hear Lula Anne come in.

"I found something," she says. "I'll try it on, and I can take it back before the store closes if you don't like it."

Course I'm gonna like it unless it's just ridiculous, I'm thinking. We've got to head out to Washington in the a.m. if we're gonna get there before Friday. Gotta make a couple stops along the way.

Lula comes in from the bedroom in about ten minutes and does a pirouette in the living room just about the time my dreamland is returning. I joggle my stiffened torso awake and think I'm looking at my fairy godmother. It's a beautiful white gown, looking almost like a wedding dress.

"It ain't gonna work," I say.

She gets this big frustrated look and is about ready to read me off when I say, "It'll take to much from Martha. They'll all be looking at you."

She gives me one of those relieved, *I caught the cat,* smiles, and says, "Got it on sale. And I can bring it back for a seventy-five percent refund. It's like renting it. Don't know when I'd ever wear it again, so I'm going to do it."

So we pack the dress, my boots, gas up the Wrangler and we're off to Washington on the following day. Got one, maybe two stops along the way.

CHAP 6. Leaving for Washington

It's about a week before we're supposed to be there but I've got some people I want to visit in South Carolina on the way. Jack Ripple is a buddy of mine from the service and we've always kept in touch. He and his wife, Alma lives out on Lake Murray, next to the water with all the amenities. Once a year or so, we've been going there for a few days, and he Alma come down here to Florida to do the same. Things to do for all of us in both places.

When they're here, we take them to all the tourist traps, which in Florida are pretty numerous, then out to Sonny's or somewhere where they can get some barbeque. Jack can never seem to get enough barbeque.

They like to go out to The Villages, an adult community on the way back from the airport. There's some little shops, a golf course, a bandstand where you can hear music and dance almost all day long. A movie theater with cheap tickets. Houses all around. Fun to watch the cars dodging in and out of the golf carts. Wonder there ain't more accidents. Everyone drives a golf cart back and forth to where they live. Just up the road aways, is a Wal-Mart and all the usual stuff, shopping and the like. They don't have nothing like it near where they live unless they drive for half an hour into Columbia. So they really like to come here and enjoy something different with us.

We live just up the road apiece in Ocala. Got a big doublewide in a resort-like community. Gated and all, surrounded by a coupla golf courses. One's got about a five-hole replica of the Masters. They usually come winters. You don't want to be here summers.

When we're there, they take us out on the lake, fishing and boating around to some special coves where there's some quaint restaurants specializing in almost everything. Then we'll tour the beachfront homes, there's a lot of big ones, in his pontoon boat, and head back to the place for a afternoon cocktail and barbeque.

Jack's part Cherokee and was raised in North Carolina. Near the old tribal lands as he tells it. He's a little older than me, and during World War II was one of the guys using Indian code to transmit messages at the Pacific front after D-Day. That's what he tells me anyways. I thought only the Navajos did it, but I don't want to dig too deep and hurt our friendship. Sometimes he's a little sensitive about being corrected about anything.

Remember once, he asked my opinion about 9/11. I answered by saying I was just as concerned about all the deaths we have on the highways every year, *by choice*. He's patriotic and don't like my answer, so he's sullen for a while but eventually gets over it. Not one to hold a grudge. Just takes it different than the rest of us sometimes. Me too, I guess. Anyways, he was my gunnery sergeant in The Korean War that I was in.

That's another thing I want to do while I'm in Washington—visit the new Korean War Memorial. It's about time there was one there for us. Every other war got one before we did. I wonder what they'll erect for Desert Storm? Probably a oilrig. That's what my brother Ray says they were trying to save in the first place.

"Every bit of foreign oil we save," he says, "is oil we don't have to dig out of Texas and Oklahoma. I know, I know," he says, " production is important to the American economy. But conservation is more important in the long run." He must have read too many environmental books. Probably Al Gore's. Gets his ideas from a lot of places.

Ray's deep; too deep for me. Remember when we was kids back in Nevada, he got pissed off on a trip we took up to the Salmon

River on the way to Jackpot. While I opened gates to drive back into the upper part of the river, he'd be telling me about all the shit he saw in the beaver ponds as we went. Real turds I'm talkin' about. And he'd say how the farmers had leased all these lands from the government for pittance, put up fences, then let their cattle use this river and a lot like it all over the state, to pollute it with cow shit.

"What about the wild horses, coyotes, cougars and the beavers themselves?" I questioned it all.

"Yeah, but the environment can take it from them," he says. "There's not enough of them to ruin it. It gets oxidized in a hurry and remains almost as clean as where it starts in the Jarbidge Mountains."

I supposed he's right, but there's nothing in Nevada that seemed to me worth the keeping. I mean, lookit history. Didn't everyone just use Nevada for a place to wander through to get somewhere else? It's always been used like a temporary stop. Get there, take what you need or want, and get out.

There's better states to live in. Like Florida, for instance. All the water we want. Flows right out of the ground on its own. We don't even bother to tap into the flowing stuff, there's so much already left underground.

But Ray says it's gonna happen here too, and not too long from now. He might be right, but I'm guessing someone'll figure out how to get more before that happens. Did I tell you

Ray's tight with a buck? He's always quoting Ben Franklin about saving a penny or something like that.

***

We're about ready to leave for South Carolina the following day when Lula Anne stops me.

"I forgot," she says, "Two things. Cat and shoes."

The first I understand. Never give it a thought until now, myself. The second is something I've gotten used to over the years.

"If you can ask Smitty, I'll be back soon's I can. Maybe Payless has some to go with this dress."

"Can't it wait till South Carolina?" I say.

"I know the stores here now. Besides, I don't want to have to drive all the way into town and waste the Ripples' time."

"Okay," I say, and get away from the Wrangler and go over to Smitty's. She peels down the street like a madwoman, which is not too unusual to see. Kids and dogs better get outta the way. Tried to tell her umpteen times that this was a ten-mile speed limit place.

"No one drives ten miles an hour around here," she says. She's always had a heavy foot. Me, I'm the one that's always had the accidents. I don't think she's got any on her record. *Moving violations* the DMV calls mine. I go next door to ask a favor from Smitty.

"Gonna stay in the Lincoln Room?" Smitty asks as I write down everything to do with the cat. "No need to write it Ed, he says. We done it before, you know."

"I don't know where," I say. "Knowing Ray, we'll probably have to share a bedroom with him and Maartha." I keep reminding myself how frugal Ray is. Lula'd like me using that word.

Ray was tight about everything when we was growing up. I remember him patching his socks with thread just so's he could always have six pair, neatly rolled in a row in his bureau drawer. Then would come his skivvies, rolled up too. He was a G.I. before he was eligible to be one officially. Be sewing at a hole in a sock fit over a light bulb. Hell, we wasn't even poor. He's probably got those same socks hidden in a trunk somewhere in the White House.

"Where do they store stuff in the White House?" I ask Smitty out loud.

"Huh?" he answers. I didn't even know I said it. He looks at me funny. "Thought we were talking about where you and Lula were going to stay?" he says.

"Oh, uh . . . yuh, the Lincoln Room, I bet."

"Well say hello to George and Martha," he says, as I get ready to leave.

I twist my face at 'im. Can't figure out how he forgot Ray's name so fast. Then he says, "You know, George and Martha Washington?"

"Ha, right."

Say hello to their ghosts. I'll bet they're around somewhere. Then I mosey on home to wait for Lula Anne to get back from the store so we can get started.

I'm thinking all the while, has Smitty got something confused? Does he mean to be talking about Abe and Mary Todd? Why does he change the subject suddenly to George and Martha? Maybe he meant to say Ray? I suppose old George wouldn't mind us staying there though. Was there even a White House when he was president? I don't think so.

Later, when I talk to Lula Ann while she's looking over her e-mail, I ask, "Can you find out about Lincoln's wife on the Internet?"

"Sure, why?" she asks.

"Was her name Martha?"

Now I'm getting confused. But I can't really remember if I'm sure about Lincoln's wife's name. Is it Martha?

"Mary," she says.

"Okay, I trust you," I say, "but to be sure, can you dig something up?"

She finds a web page, and scrolls down some facts. There's the one I'm looking for. I have her print it out for me. Here's what it says:

"Lincoln married Mary Todd on November 4. James Harvey Matheny was the best man. Abraham gave Mary a gold wedding ring with the words 'Love is Eternal' engraved inside the band. Mary wore this ring until the day she died. The marriage took place in the parlor of the Edwards' home, and the ceremony was performed by Reverend Charles Dresser, an Episcopal minister. The Lincolns moved into the Globe Tavern, a two story wooden structure in Springfield, where they boarded for $4.00 a week."

So there it was. Her name really was Mary. Someone's put together a whole lot of stuff on Lincoln, and I thank him for it.

CHAP 7. On the road again

I'm watching the morning news when Lula comes in the door. "Shhh," I say, "something's up with Ray."

CNN is reporting that there's a plot by the Iranians, they think, to possibly assassinate my brother that's just been discovered. The National Security Council, FBI and the CIA have just moved in and taken him to safety.

The broadcaster, Jim Henning, reads and announces, " . . . and moments ago the President and First Lady were taken to an undisclosed location, along with the Vice president and his family, to a different location. The White house reports that the terrorist plot may be widespread, a large front, and investigators are proceeding to the New York area and other cities along the Atlantic shores from New York to Virginia.

"One moment please . . . we've just received news that the United States Coast Guard is on alert and patrolling the Atlantic waters along this same section of coastline. We now switch to reporter Billy Buff Dixon who is on the boardwalk in Atlantic City for an update. Billy, can you see anything as you look out on the waters of the Atlantic? What is the vantage offering from where you are?"

"What's happening?" Lula puts her shoebox on the table and sits at the front edge of the living room recliner.

"It just came on," I say. "I was watching our recent bombing in the Tehran desert. Suddenly they switched to this news."

"Are we still going?" she asks.

"Well, I don't know now. I suppose we can still go far's Sou' Carolina. He knows where we're stopping, so I suppose he can get in touch to tell us what further to do."

"Now Ed, how's he going to be able to get in touch with us with all those body guards? Are we being invaded or what?"

"How in hell do I know?"

I'm irritated. The first time we've had a invite to the White House and this happens.

"We're probably better off there than here. At least they've got some hills and trees we can hide in if we're being attacked. Better'n this flat palm tree stuff not too far from the Cape. They'll probably be sending missiles to knock out our stuff around there. Next thing you know, they'll be blowing up the manatees in Crystal River thinking they're miniature submarines."

"Quit talking silly," she says. Course she's right. Sometimes my brain runs away using my mouth for transportation. Gets lost and wants to come home, too. In the meantime we're glued right here in the living room.

We watch the news for another hour. A special report comes on every third channel, all feeding the same news we heard in the first five minutes. By noon, the pundits will be on, and they'll be analyzing this and that, making it all sound like the Second World War's with us again. I recognize a few faces that been analyzing every conflict for the last umpteen years. They sound the same as they always have. Shoulda made a recording and just filled in different names and faces.

"Okay, let's go," I say. "We can listen on the car radio."

"Want to bring that small portable black and white?" she says.

"If you want." I'm just wishing at the time that she *would* ask.

"How you like these?" she opens the shoebox and slips a shoe on her right foot. It's a tiny thing, white with gold trim, with about a medium heel. "I didn't want high ones. Didn't know how long we might have to stand in a reception line."

"Probably not at all," I say. "You think

we're going to be dignitaries or something?"

"Well, could be. Ma-aar-tha told me a few things about the guest list. Says she was going to surprise Ray with a few eminent people from the music and art world at his performance."

"Oh, I'll bet he'll like that. You know how he likes surprises. Hhrumph," I add.

Ray never did like it when anything happened that he didn't plan or know about. That's what was so surprising to us all when he decided to go into politics. Hell, there's surprises all the time there. Even at that, he's always acted calm in adjusting to anything new that came up, including my sister-in-law's exercise videos. I'll bet he was fuming the night all the news reports played excerpts of her grunting and grinding on a foam pad. But he adjusted right away. It had been all a surprise to him. He didn't even know she was making it. Made the final scenes out at Camp David too. Ha, we all laughed about that. We'd see him get out of the helicopter on the White House lawn, and he'd be alone.

"Yes, she's fine," Ray'd tell reporters on the ground as he walked away from the chopper.

"Want to get the place picked up and get an extra day," she'd tell him. Then the cameras'd roll in, and start taping.

"I'm glad the First Lady is setting an example for the rest of our nations youth, specially the women," he'd answer the first question at his news conference.

"Sure Ray, like you knew it all along,"
I'd talk to the TV.

Lula puts the shoe back in the box and
we're ready to go.

"Cat all taken care of?" she says.

I nod.

"Pull the plugs on the computer and
TV's?"

I nod again.

"Okay, I guess that's it then. Smiths'
know where the key is kept, right?"

"Same as last time?" I ask.

"Uh-huh. Let's go then."

We get to the corner of the street and she
says, "Let's stop at Winn-Dixie. One more
thing."

I've long since gotten used to the routine
and don't protest or refuse. I turn into the parking lot.

In minutes, she's out with another bag.
When she's in her seat belt again she hands me
my own water bottle as I'm pulling onto the
highway. I'm hoping this'll end it.

In ten minutes we're on the old road
where we'll connect with the interstate to Jacksonville, up ol' highway 301. Used to be the
main route through central Florida till the interstate took over.

We hardly talk when we're on the road.
She's thinking all the time and so am I, but on
two different channels. She takes out a book
and opens to a marked page. Me, I'm thinking

about what's happening to Ray and the Washington gang.

I hate to disturb her, but I'm anxious to bring out the black and white TV that's sitting on the back seat, under the too-late-to-pack clothes we threw in at the last minute. We'll probably leave them that way so's to hide the TV from potential thieves. Yeah, like somebody wants an old portable black and white, twelve volt only, TV.

"Will the radio bother you?" I say, reaching for the knob.

"No."

I press the SEEK button a few times till news comes on. A commentator is reporting the same stuff we heard on TV about an hour ago. I tune in three or four more stations then click it off. Meanwhile, she hasn't missed a word in her reading.

"You don't really care, do you?" I say.

"About what?" she looks at me, thumbing her place at the same time.

"About Ray and the rest of the country."

"Now why would you say a thing like that?" she says.

"Well, here we are, in possibly the biggest national crisis since he took office, and you don't even want to watch the news."

"Course I care," she says. "Do you want me to bring the TV up front?"

"Well, I thought you'd have it on by now."

"No, I didn't want it to distract you. Remember what happened during the Super Bowl?"

She's right of course, like she usually is. We was coming home from I can't remember where. Oh yeah, from a trip back home. When we drove back from Orlando, the Super Bowl was on. I took my eyes off to watch a touchdown pass replay that I had missed while my eyes were on the road, and screeched into a ditch beside the turnpike. Cost us three hundred bucks for that pull out and tow, not to mention the replacement of a wheel and some other stuff that got torn up.

She plugs it into the cigarette lighter receptacle and sets it on the glove compartment lid.

"Now, just listen, okay?" she says. "If you wanna watch, just pull into a rest stop for a while, and I can read, okay?"

I don't answer. No more fuel for the fire, my thinking.

CHAP 8. Trip continued . . .

"Denny's okay?" I ask. I begin to turn in when she stops me.

"I don't like their attitude toward Blacks," she says.

I swerve the hood back into the right lane, get tooted at by an irate follower and get about half way through Starke when she signals that a Pizza Hut'll be just fine.

"A Pizza Hut? When do you stop at Pizza Huts?" I say.

"Right now," she answers.

I'm thinking if I brought some Rolaids with me. Can't wait for afternoon indigestion to start. The parking lot outside looks almost deserted. Across the street there's a McDonald's, a Burger King two blocks down, a Taco Bell about a block in the opposite direction. Any of these I would prefer over a Pizza Hut.

Anyway we park and go in. Inside we order some pan-sized individual pizzas with a side of Pepsi.

Twenty minutes goes by and the food still ain't here. About halfway through our wait, Lula gets up to use the restroom. In the meantime, I've loaded up with two Pepsi refills. TV on the wall is blaring the same news that we saw earlier in the morning. A few new clips shows Ray and Maartha, three poodles and a large gray cat joining them in boarding a helicopter.

I'm trying to listen, but interference is coming from a family in the next booth doing rehearsals for the zupper train at Disney Land, or Disney World, or whatever. I can never remember the right names for the East Coast or West Coast variety. Meanwhile, the music from the ceiling is screaming over everything, some hip-hop stuff that I can't stand, even if it's the first time I've heard it. Pizza Hut? What in hell made her choose this?

Lula gets back to the table just as our two pans arrive. By now, I'm so full of Pepsi, I could take mine to go. But she insists that I stay while she eats hers.

"They're messy," she says.

I already know the implication. No need to grease up the seats in the car.

When we're done, we wait another ten minutes for someone to bring the check. Twice, this waitress comes to the table to tell us she's going to bring it right away. She walks by about four times in between, then goes back to the kitchen, stopping by the restroom on about the third time. When the restroom door opens, I can see a cloud trailing her as she leaves. She's had a quick smoke and stops to pick up her next order. The first time she stops with the check, she discovers she's added wrong, and returns to the kitchen for repairs. When she comes back she's got it right, and apologizes all over us about the delay.

"We've been so busy today," she says. "I can't wait for this shift to end," she smiles, a wad of gum switches from left cheek to right.

Busy. Yeah, right. There's two tables filled besides ours, and it's only eleven thirty a.m. Wonder what she'll do during the real lunch hour. Probably hide in the bathroom, where her stash of cancer sticks is waiting.

When we get to the parking lot, two guys are rapping, one with his elbow on my car hood, the other with one foot propped up on my front bumper. I don't want to start anything right now, so I try not to look at them while I unlock the car door. Lula is getting ready for a full frontal attack, but I glare a "no contact" look at her and she gets in, all the while, giving them a dagger stare-down. They ignore her. When I start the engine, the one on the bumper waits a second, then tosses me a frustrated look, implying my audacity at infringing on his concentration. He brings his foot to the ground and casually steps out of the way. The one on the hood follows his lead, and both take a standing position that allows their T-shirts to brush along the sides of the car when I back out.

I didn't have a chance to wash the car before we left, so I can picture the look we're gonna get from other drivers on the road, when they see a horizontal clean stripe along the length of the car as we drive. Probably start a new trend. Don't wash the entire car, folks. Leave some stripes in between the dirt. It's a new fad. I can see opening a car wash business now. First, they mask off a portion of the car you don't want washed. Next they buff everything dry, and peel off the masked section. Charge you an extra two bucks for what they didn't wash.

In my heyday, those goons would a had to take a pointy toe boot in the ass, no matter how many times I had to pick myself up off the ground to do it. Not now. The only thing I've got going is a lawsuit against them for hitting a senior. What good is that going to do me if I'm laid up in the hospital for six months and have to walk with a cane for the rest of my life? I'm trying to relate the actions of those two kids to my own when I was that age. Did I do that kind of dumb stuff? I suppose I did, but it sure seems remote and inoffensive to me now.

CHAP 9. Stumbles; but the trip is still on

We continue up the highway that used to be a main route through central Florida. Some of the old tourist traps still survive, but most are gone. We just passed one, a big red sign advertising T-shirts and orange juice. We run by a motel that used to be a tourist-grabber, but now caters mostly to daytime construction workers. Try to get a non-smoking room in one of those.

It's mostly a boring drive through pine trees and palmetto. In about an hour we connect with Interstate 10, the main road between Jacksonville and the panhandle. Now the real driving challenge begins. Truckers pass on both sides, or gang in two's in passing lanes to make road signs invisible until the last minute. Do

they plan it that way? Nah, the mentality can't be there.

Lula is finishing her book when we begin the loop around Jacksonville. I managed to duck into the left lane just in time to make the turn north-bound. She looks up, but don't ask where we are. She wants to, but something holds her back, so she turns in her seat, puts the spent book in a bag on the back seat and extracts another one. "Hungry?" I ask.

"We just ate," she says.

"That was an hour and a half ago."

"I'm not hungry."

"Okay. Gotta get gas before too long. Stop just over the line."

"Hmmm." She opens the new reading material and sinks her head after readjusting her seat. She don't bite.

There's a string of gas stations just over the Georgia line that sells gas real cheap as compared to about any place in the country. I remember it from the times we been up here before. I look at my gauge again and hope I'll make it all the way. I was gonna fill it before we left, but figured I could make it until we got here. Damn, now I'm a little worried.

"Gas up?" she asked before we left.

I didn't answer, pretending like I didn't hear her, all the while thinking that I could fill up over the Georgia line, like I'm planning to do right now. She didn't pursue an answer, so I let it ride. Now she'll really be pissed if we run out of gas before getting there. I can just see her in her new white shoes, out by the highway thumbing a ride with an empty water jug in her hand. Not that I haven't done it plenty.

As a kid, we was always stretching it on some deserted Nevada dirt road. Get down to some fishing hole, fish all day and when we'd get ready to leave, find the gas tank almost empty. All the while, Ray and me studying the gage on the way coming, neither one suggesting that we fill up. Usually spend the night right there and hope some other fisherman knows about the spot.

I remember one time, when me and Ray and another kid, walked seven miles with only a Desert water bag dripping, out to the highway before we get a ride to Elko. No hats. We was burned toasty and Ray only had enough money to call our mother to come pick us up.

When we drove back to get the pickup, someone had been there and shot two holes through the windshield with a .22 rifle. We spent half the day combing the area trying to find the bastard, before mom persuaded us to empty the gas can in the truck and get out of there. Even if we got them, we didn't know what we were gonna do next. All the while, I'm saying it's probably some old time Diggers getting even with the white man, and Ray is saying that I'm just a bigoted camel and even if it was true, that payback was certainly in arrears by now.

I couldn't believe him. I just know if we found them he wouldn't have let them off that easy. I remember him pissed off a few times, and giving the bad guys their due.

Now he's the President. How did it get to be that way? He never even seemed interested in a job like that. It's not like he woke up one day in the top bunk and said, *"Ed, mark my word—someday I'm gonna be the President of the United States."* Hell, if he'd-a-said it like that, I mighta believed him. Whatever he'd set his mind to, as I've said before, he done. But when the time came, he didn't. Just one thing fell in at a time, and the first thing I know, he's headed up for the New Hampshire primary. I'm still trying to figure the image.

I gotta tell ya, Ray's not that pretty, and can be pretty boring when you get to know him real good. I'll bet Maartha'll tell you the same. Only, anything that's not in her sights is pretty boring to her.

If you'd meet Ray on the street and wasn't paying attention, you'd never recognize him as *the* President. There's absolutely nothing special about his looks. After that Clinton guy, I guess the public didn't want another lover-boy image in the White House. Well, they didn't get one with Ray. He looks pretty ordinary, like George Bush, someone like that. Course ol' George does look a little like that cartoon guy on the cover of MAD magazine once in a while. Hope Lula didn't hear me think that. Think she voted for 'im. Anyways, with a hat on and in a crowd, you'd hardly know Ray was around. His voice is even, nothing distinctive about it. Just ordinary. He's an even six foot, about the same size as every other man from the West. Slight balding; a couple of faded spots on his face, probably more now since I haven't seen him for about a year. I know they always do make-up on television. I know it because, I remember right where the spots were, and I don't see them when he's on TV. When he's not in a suit, he just wears plaid, like we all did back home and could come from just about anywhere.

That's Ray. Mr. Ordinary. And for the most part, that's about how his presidency has been. Another Eisenhower was how they tabbed him on the platform. A compromiser. Seldom brought attention to himself. More known for the trouble he didn't get us in to. That's why we're having all that trouble with Iran now I think. They think Ray's soft. I mean to tell them—he ain't soft. Don't get his dander up. I've witnessed what he can do if he's pushed too far. I remember . . . ah, there's the turnoff to the gas station. I better turn off the ignition and coast in. Naw, better not get Lula in a fade.

CHAP 10. And onward . . .

Dollar ninety-two cents a gallon. In California right now, they're paying almost three dollars. Where's the refineries in Georgia? They're all in California. Yet they pay more than the folks here. Wish I had a brought a extra five-gallon can. Then Lula'd be worried about us getting rear-ended and blown up in a auto accident. While we're both in the hospital in intensive care, she's writing me notes across the room saying, "I told you so."

Reminds me, better sign up for that extra part D on Medicare pretty soon. That's another thing I wanna address later on. Maybe when my thoughts about it have it all better figured.

Back to what I was saying about costs

being out of line. Just like groceries. Go to the store. In Florida, right next to orange groves, you buy oranges for the same as you'd pay in Colorado. In California, avocados are just as expensive as in Detroit. Makes no sense at all. The cheapest you can buy is from South America, even with import duties, shipping costs and union workers unloading at the docks. Cheaper if they come doused with pesticides.

Like I suppose our government has been keeping a eye on that too. The FDA is changing their minds all the time about stuff like that. They approve a drug after studying it for five years and in two weeks time, with adverse publicity, it gets pulled off the market. Where do they get these guys and gals from? One of the first things I remember Ray saying after he took office and had to consider the head honchos in the FDA: *"Where's Koop when you need him?"*

I been meaning to talk to Ray about all this stuff, but he'll probably tell me it's more complicated than I'm making out. Always did. He's a nuance person.

Remembered that word from a Scrabble game we played at the place we're going. Jeeze, I hope they don't bring that out again. I'm just plain no good at it.

Anyhow, Ray wants to see three sides of everything. The more he understands, the more wishy-washy he gets with an opinion.

Me, I guess I formed mine years ago. There's just some right and wrong to everything. Lula's more like Ray. When I bark at the decisions made by Congress on TV she ends up explaining to me why she thinks what they did was right. Not with everything, of course. I think that's why she made out so good with her schooling. Me, I did never see the necessity of taking all those subjects in school if you wasn't interested in something. Her—she liked everything she took, including a drafting course in high school. Tell me, what's she gonna do with a drafting course in her life? Not like she's going to plan a house to build for us.

Though, I gotta admit, she sure surprised one fella in Nevada when we made plans for our first house. She wanted the floor plan turned around ass-backwards so the sun would rise in the kitchen. He was reluctant, and said it would involve costs, materials, extra labor and all. She said she could reverse the plan and put a room different by drawing him some sketches overnight. He wasn't about to be undone by a woman. She got it her way. No extra cost neither.

We're on the road again and Lula's back inside her book. She offered to drive, but I said I wasn't ready to give it up yet. "*Now* are you hungry?" I say.

"In about an hour?" she replies.

"Okay." And put the autopilot on seventy-five. The highway patrol seems to be all right with about five miles over the limit. When I do though, seems like everyone is passing. So I do about ten over and manage to stay up.

TV in the car on again. Now they've got

Ray at some undisclosed location and the news media is doing their pundit stuff on every channel. I'll bet I know what Ray told them when they started all this stuff. *"First let's analyze the significance of it all,"* he probably began. Next he'd tell them why he was probably being targeted. *"It's only symbolic,"* he'd say. *"What they really want to impress us with is the fact that with all modern technology, anyone, including the leader of the most powerful nation on earth is an acceptable target. They really don't care if they get me or not. That they place a hit on the White House is what's important."*

Like that *Muss-oo-ee* feller up for trial now, acting like his own defense attorney. I know I ain't saying his name right. What a kook. Can't wait to be put to death and get his share of all them virgins in heaven before they run out. What're they got up there, a breeding farm like Hitler used to have? *Sorry, Mrs. Alibaba, it's a boy. We're going to have to send it to China. Remember now,* girls only *from now on.*

Ray's continuing his response in my head: *"Not just a hit either, but major destruction like we did to the president of Yugoslavia's home in Belgrade in nineteen and ninety-nine."* He was still saying dates and times like daddy said when we was kids.

"Let's stay right here," he'd say, *"Not in the White house, but somewhere nearby, maybe West Virginia. That way we can monitor moves. I'm easy to create a double for. Hell, put a mus-*

tache on me and hand me a fishing pole with a matching hat and put me on the Potomac. Nobody'll even guess."

But the CIA wouldn't have it. Naw . . . whisk him away in Air Force One. Ray's probably barking at them about missing his concert before his friends, his kin, and the nation on Sunday night.

Right now, Lula and me's just about given up on Saturday. Will probably be glued to the TV while playing a thousand games of Mucker with Jack and Alma while we sip at new brands of beer on the screened porch. Hope they can keep the Scrabble packed away. Maybe I can find it soon's we get there and hide it under our bed. They'll never think of looking for it there.

That's the Ripples' latest hobby. They go out and buy exotic beers from microbreweries blooming all over creation and spring them upon visiting guests. That's us.

I don't know where they're taking Ray and family, but they'll probably regret it. It'll be the "Ransom of Red Chief" all over, only this time it'll be the *Ransom of Maartha.* He can't be confined too long anymore neither. Used to have patience about that stuff, but not anymore. Washington's got him ruined by now. Always has to be doing something. Hope he can let down easy-like when the fifteen minutes of fame is over.

Even if he's reading he can't sit still. His mind's always ahead of the line. Where did this and that thought come from? Ah yes, he'd say aloud often times. We'd all look up from what we was doing and there he'd be, writing some note or copying a quotation from a book.

I've got news for you boys. Put the hat on 'im and give him the pole. You don't want 'im around you right now. But y'all'll be busy enough with Maartha. Maybe she'll have time to give him aerobic lessons first-hand for a while.

Just as we're ready to pull into a Cracker Barrel, a flash comes on. Some reporter is telling about an unofficial report of the Pentagon tracking a submarine off the coast near North Carolina. It's Russian, and they've supposedly been tracking it, as it's zigzagged across the Atlantic since it left the Azores about a month ago. Nothing's verified and there's more news to follow.

In the meantime, they switch back to Jerry Springer. It's the only channel we can get right now. Lula hates it but I think it's a new kind of entertainment. After being in Florida for a while, it's pretty close to real life as I see it. Let me say what's going on right now: Two gals, in their mid-twenties have just been re-seated from fighting for the third time. Both are about a hundred pounds overweight, one has a wig on that's already been ripped off twice. So she's fit it on her head best she can and it looks ridiculous. The other has three teeth missing on one side and loves to smile. They're seated once again and Jerry's getting to introduce what they been fighting over. Microphones have been re-adjusted—on one, there's only a strand of bra left to pin it on. The technician is taking his time. They call out the boyfriend who comes on, doing a little jig, and when he takes his hat off, he's bald and about ninety years old. What a stud!

"You coming in or not?" Lula says, bent over, peeping through the top of the window that I haven't quite got all the way up yet.

"I'm behind you, " I say.

CHAP 11. Restaurant stop

Cracker Barrel is designed to resemble an old time store. Food predominantly Country. On the way in you stumble through aisles of Nashville-type tack, barely sitting on the shelves, waiting for some little kid to crash to the floor. *"That'll be seventeen dollars and thirty-nine cents,"* a clerk says as the child's father admonishes the kid for knocking it off the shelf. In the meantime, the little one is picking through the jellies on the floor that were excised as part of the original package. Don't matter that some are impregnated with glass. Just a short drive to the nearby medical facility in Savanna. Before the day is over, a short stop at the local Cracker Barrel will run to nine thousand and seventy-five dollars. "Rounded," the billing notice will say. "We can drop the odd cents." It's a Southern thing. A few wandering turns through the aisles, and Lula is ready to eat.

"It's over here," I say, having found the entrance to the dining room. Is there another way out I'm thinking? No way.

Waitress brings water and asks about coffee. Water automatic. Difference between East and West. Last time we were home, what I call Nevada, restaurant's service stopped serving water automatically, except for the finest. It's a premium there, like it's always been.

Someone told me, or I read it, that over ninety percent of the potable supply in the U.S. is east of the Mississippi. Probably true. What's going to get it on this side is pollution. All them wells down in Florida, pumping from the aquifer.No regulation. Fly-by-night well mechanics. Erosion, incursion, intrusion, all the words that help pollute the big underground lake. Matter of time. Everyone's drinking from plastic now anyway. Don't mind bathing with PVCs; just don't want to inhale.

Lula took a six-pack of water bottles with us. Me, I took a drink before we left. Heard George Carlin say it one night on a TV special, not exactly the same way as I just did.

Water cost more'n a gallon of gas before she got out of the store. Imagine, a bottle of water where it's all made, costing like a gallon of gas. Something's wrong somewhere. I'll have to talk with Ray about this. Our monthly phone conversations. Better write it down.

I take a pad out of my pocket and begin to make a note. Lula has got up from the table in the meantime and is back in the main entrance room looking over the books on tape that Cracker Barrel rents. Guess it ain't all bad. My second cup of coffee has arrived, but still no sign of someone to take our food order.

When Lula gets back with two tapes, she says, "Order?" I say I'll take the eggs over easy and a side of country ham.

She don't even crack a smile. Sometimes, I wonder where my humor drifts. Lost, like the abandoned mines of Jarbidge. That's a old ghost town up near where we used to live. Actually some new would-be ghosts are comin' alive and beginning to inhabit the place once again. I hope not. That used to be my favorite place to go on Fourth of July. Soon's someone discovers it, tells his friends who tell their friends, it'll all be ruined like everything else. Too many people anymore just trying to find the right place to go exclusive of the tourist crowd. When they get there, they find Boy Scout troops. Privacy anymore is at home and a TV set. Vacation time the same way.

The waitress finally shows up and I order a sandwich. Lula asks about bagels, She-Crab soup, then to the waitress' relief, orders same as me. I'm gonna ask about the soup when the little gal leaves.

"She-Crab soup? When do you eat She-Crab soup?" I say. "Ain't no such thing, I bet."

"Is too," she says. "Want the recipe?"

"Betcha five."

"You're on," she says, and begins to scribble the recipe on a napkin. We go through lots of napkins on bets like this. I think she's ahead of me in the winnings.

"Now," she says, "if you don't have access to the crab roe, which you may not, since you're not suppose to catch them in the first place, you substitute egg yolks. That'll be five," she sticks out a paw. She wouldn't have gone through all this if it wasn't true. Not her style. I reach in my pocket, pull out my clip and peel off five ones.

"Don't you have a fiver?" she says.

Now I'm not about to operate deeper for her convenience seeing she's probably snookered me. So I fold the clip quick-like back into my pocket.

"Spends the same," I say.

It's been about forty-five minutes and the food finally gets here. The waitress sets it down and leaves before asking the magic question. I have to wait another five minutes before I can catch her eye to bring the condiments. Specially the horseradish. Now I've got a cold roast beef.

Lula's reading the jackets to the tapes and is already half done eating. I wolf mine to catch up. She notices. "You'll be squirming," she says. She's right too. When I eat too fast these days, it seems to just stay there forever. Then the pain just stays on my left side until somehow a gallon of water or so later it gradually disappears.

I've taken to not drinking when I eat. Someone somewhere says it's better to let the digestive juices dissolve the food first, that is, if it's been taken in small enough bites and chewed like hell before swallowing. Why didn't that seem to affect me like this when I was younger? I remember coming in from all day in the saddle after daddy bought that ranch at Wild Horse and eating everything in sight just before bedtime. Sleep like a baby, get up the next morning and ask, "What's for breakfast?"

Exercise. That's the difference. Bet Maartha don't have my problems, with all her aerobic stuff. Wonder what she's gonna do right now with her and Ray on the run. The girls off at college too. They'll have some classes to make up, I bet.

What's with these presidents with all these girls? Nixon, Carter, Clinton. Regan and Ford had boys, but they were already grown while their folks was in the White House. Be fun to see a boy going through the gymnastics of being raised in the White House while his father's the Pres. Drive the secret service crazy.

"Who's that you have with you this evening Mr. Smith?" a guard would challenge. "It's my best friend, Bobby Jones," the lad answers. "He's visiting overnight." In the guise of Bobby Jones, a young lady's hair is stuffed under a baseball cap; she's wearing baggie Levi's and a plaid wool shirt, probably one of the president's favorites. "Very well sir, you may proceed," and salutes the president's son with a wave, to continue toward the opposite end of the White House.

Not that the girls haven't been as clever. I'll bet those Johnson girls got around more'n the old man thought. And Margaret. She had Harry's number too. Was just like him. If she'd a got caught with some of her escapades, she would've come right out and said, "The buck stops here, Father, I admit to having a little romance on the side." Then again, she was probably too busy doing her Maria Callas stuff to get into too much Dutch.

We're done and get up to leave. "Got a tip?" I say. She knows I know. Now I get a little even for being taken with the She-Crab. She digs out two of the ones I give her and puts them under the cup. But she's being good on the way out. Doesn't stop to check any more aisles or lift some of the nearby do-dads.

"How's ever'thin'?" the clerk asks as I hand her a twenty.

"Fine," I lie, grabbing a mint and a toothpick.

"What about the tapes?" she says, looking at Lula who's still reading one of the jackets.

"Already got 'em," I say.

The girl nods and hands me some change. On the way out, we each try one of the easy rockers lined up on the porch for everyone to trip on as they walk by. "Got to get something for the Ripples'," she says.

"A rocker?"

"No dummy, not a rocker. Some wine maybe."

Right, like Jack and Alma are gonna stray from their beer. Neither one'd know wine if it was served at a Baptist communion. Which it ain't. "Gee Alma, this is sure fine grape juice," Jack'd say.

CHAP 12. A conspiracy

While I'm telling all about the road trip to visit with our friends and go to the White House to see Ray, something's been festering in the background all this time that started back about a year ago, as I find out later. I'm gonna take you there now. I'll try to tell it like it was told me.

Simon Lasting, U.S. Navy retired, is about to come out of mothballs from his residence in Post Falls, Idaho. Once weekly, he gets together with other retirees from the neighborhood, mostly police officers from Los Angeles and New Orleans for the ritual poker game. This week he's acting and playing strange. Has miss-called two big pots already and the evening has just begun.

"That meeting really got to you," a player reminds him.

The meeting he's referring to is one held on the shores of Lake Pend Oreille the weekend prior. Leaders of the Aryan Movement, Northwest, has asked him to deliver a speech about some of America's wrongs and the direction in which it was headed. Ex-Commander Lasting was happy to oblige.

He starts his speech low-key, but in the heat of the moment, it becomes personal. He suddenly throws his notes aside, begins to ad lib in ambiguous terms concerning his personal problems with the Navy; his requested resignation, for what he thought to be a necessary situation aboard a submarine in the discipline of his men; and the unfairness of the Pentagon; its wishy-washy attitude about men in the field and the like. He thought he would receive the same kind of response he had gotten so many times before when he had delivered a similar planned speech to a diverse group, but to his surprise, nearly everyone there yielded a sympathetic ten minute standing ovation. He was reminded of it still the next day, rubbing sore muscles from all the pats on the back received in an impromptu reception line the day before.

The following day his phone vibrates synchronously with nerve endings attempting to restore themselves at skin level. The major thrust is an offer for a new submarine command. No, it did not originate at the Pentagon.

"I've got a little thinking to do, if you

guys don't mind, I'll cash in," he informed other players about an hour into the game.

"He's not feeling well, I can tell," the man to the right of the vacated space spoke as he dealt the next hand.

This guy turns out to be a plant, as I later put it all together.

"He needs a woman," the man to the left of the space added.

"Never saw him with one, has anybody?" None could recall.

In the middle of the night, Commander Lasting packs his old duffle, a flexible cloth suitcase, leaves a note for his housemaid, extra food for the two cats, and calls a cab to take him to the airport in Spokane.

At O'Hare in Chicago, two men, with instructions, greet him, and before he boards a flight to France, one hands him an identity and passport. He can still turn back, but decides to continue.

Two days later, six men, half sporting shaved heads, take him by boat from Dieppe to a submarine waiting in the Channel near England. He's applauded on arrival as he climbs down the hatch ladder of a retrofitted Russian submarine. Most of his subordinates, some having familiar faces, greet him in English. His old legs remember new positions.

A cursory inspection of his new charge reveals that most basics are still familiar to him. In a few days he will learn all he needs to know about his new command. "Out of the channel and on toward the ridge," his first orders.

No sissies this time. He has men among him, believing in an important cause, willing to take any risk. No more boys sending home letters to their mothers about his alleged cruelties. No more investigations by superiors of inappropriate personal activities with young seamen in his quarters, or the use of rejection on their part, to provide him with cause to toughen up the whole crew. Weeks at a time below surface where the air grew stale and blood boiled for lack of adequate oxygen. This is a different crew. Last man alive surfaces, but only when scuttling is complete.

His first look through a magnifying lens over the surface above gives him pause to linger with one arm crooked over the periscope handle.

In his musing, he is at the academy, laboring over equations in a course in nuclear physics. He thought he had a handle on a normalization process that would be interesting to investigators searching for a *top* quark. For two days, almost without sleep or food, he exhausted pen and pad, finally coming to a proof he found acceptable, negativity thoroughly examined and refuted. He sent the proof to a physicist at Brookhaven. More than interest came with the reply. It was a fresh examination. An offer of future correspondence and possible publication appended the letter. Though interested, he was still an undergraduate, had miles to go, to be followed by eight years of active duty—already committed. Though a leading student in his major, nuclear physics, he was at odds with himself, mired in the capabilities of political intrigue; the influence it could have in allowing him to adjust to demands of both researcher and candidate. He simply gave permission to his correspondent to use whatever was wanted as beneficial to the cause of science. Many years later, with two additional quarks discovered, Lasting found his normalization equations crucial to the experimental confirmation. In only one instance was his work cited, as a footnote, regarding his efforts.

When Lasting lowers the periscope, he turns to meet with a slight, heavily bearded man.

"Ami ben-Abi," the man bows.

Lasting contains a handshake.

"I am here as an observer to monitor the sponsorship of my nation," he tells Lasting.

Great. Another Pentagon to contend with. Still, he realizes that funds have to come from somewhere. Already, ten million dollars has been deposited into a Swiss bank account in Lasting's name.

"I will be with you until the Azores," the man speaks in perfect English.

"Harvard?" Lasting asks.

"Princeton."

"I suppose you've decided to call the project . . .?"

"Deep Penetration," the Shiite says.

"Of course, why didn't I think of that?"

Lasting replies, then adds, "Just try to stay out of the way of the working crew."

To wit, the man bows and retires from the operations room.

As instructed, the "sponsor" is not seen in general quarters until one day before reaching the islands. When he greets Lasting with another courteous bow, he says, "Tomorrow night, a helicopter will meet us at these coordinates. Would you kindly surface at twenty-one hundred hours?" He hands Lasting a chart.

Lasting simply nods and the man returns to his quarters.

CHAP 13. Contemplating world politics

The pundits are having a radio field day. And on the small black and white, a TV day. Pundits-at-large. Articulate messengers with inaccurate hypotheses. Did I just say that? Honestly, I don't know where some of this stuff comes from sometimes. Maybe Scrabble is doing me better'n I thought.

Not since the foment of the environmental age is so much credit given to public opinion. The Iranian crisis has been ongoing for about six months. All because of some ethnic cleansing of minorities inhabiting the region near the border of Pakistan. Harmless squatters when they first arrived, they say.

The Pakistanis began building the big ones, and the Iranians got nervous. So now they're driving them out at gunpoint and we're trying to avert another ethnic cleansing, as we call it; also prevent a potential nuclear war that Pakistan is threatening. They've got their missiles zeroed on Teheran, and not loaded with buckshot either, so they say. In the meantime, they're gonna wait and see what we can do to ameliorate the situation. Lula'd like me using that last one.

About two weeks ago, there was another school shoot-'em-up. This time in Babylon, Wyoming. I didn't even know we had a Babylon in the U.S. of A. Then Lula said, "Sure there is. What about Babylon, New York?"

We keep getting names to parallel biblical settings. I suppose there's a Hell, something-or-other, and a Christ, and so forth as names of towns. Just so's they don't duplicate the reported goings on as in the Bible. Is this about history repeating itself, as they say, or are we wired to keep going with the same playback we've experienced before? I'm not sure of what I just said. Just a feeling I get sometime about living our lives like a soap opera. You know, it's the same program every day, dressed up to look like something different. That make any sense?

"Okay," I say. So she follows up on her computer and sure enough, in the last three years, a community has grown up on the downside of the mountains above Cheyenne, and decided to call itself Babylon. First developer from Babylon, New York.

The stuff you can learn these days. Course I'm still trying to find out how to open my e-mail. I leave all that stuff to Lula, since she taught school and all. She says there's some good stuff on the Internet about piano tuning and has put some on the desktop for me to look at. I have to ask her how to open the stuff up. Can't seem to remember in between times that she shows me. *Downloading* she calls it.

Some piano tuner from New Mexico has a web page and now I can find out all about tuning and repair, the age of some piano lines, a whole bunch of stuff I wish I had when I was in the business in Reno. Did I mention that was where I met Lula? Well, not exactly in Reno, but we both ended up there at the same time when the principal part of our courtship began.

Her folks had just come out from Florida and took her with them. She's an only kid. Was, that is. Still is, I guess. To me, anyways. I'll say more about that later.

Anyhow, there was a shooting at the new Babylon Middle School, just dedicated six months before. Four kids, who were supposed to be bussed down to another town for high school hung back in the early morning and began spraying kids with shot soon as they stepped off the bus. More kids killed, but less wounded than in Littleton, Colorado, 'while back.

Course in the middle of Ray's troubles,

he's now got to get on TV and answer for all that too. He's gotta act like he's against guns, but I know he's really not. Hell, without guns, we wouldn't a had no fun at all as kids. Plunking jackrabbits and sage hens was about our favorite pastime on the ranch when we wasn't digging potatoes, or sacking them, or shipping. Not to mention all the coyotes we hung on fences. Scares off the new immigrants, coyotes too. And *coyotes* also, if you get my drift. If you don't, it don't matter.

So the pundits are saying we gotta get tougher with crime. Lock up more kids. Three strikes and you're sent away forever. Regulated gun control. Build self-esteem. Parental responsibility. Curfews. Interdiction and mediation, two words I don't really know the meaning of. Prevention? No way.

And in the meantime, while this is all gonna be brought about, our leaders will set a example of *You shall not murder.* That's the real Hebrew translation, though Lula'll argue about it. Start by blowing up troops in the Iranian desert, a province called Sistan va Baluchestan, and zero in on the unofficial policy of killing off the ringleaders. Yeah, I looked that one up in my files that I cut out of the newspaper.

I'm surprised that one got through Congress. But only by two votes. It's legal they said; had biblical precedence. It's okay now to kill off guys like Milosevic and the like. Won't have to now, so I've read and heard on the news

lately. Had a *artichoke*. That's what we used to
call it back home. Yeah, right, like someone
didn't get tired of housing and feeding him in
Dutch country. Knew they'd never get him
brought to trial. Somebody's got to foot the bill
for all that justice. Maybe we refused finally,
and someone said, we'll *do him in* ourselves.
Save the expense. Like putting down a horse
that ain't no use anymore. In spite of what he
done to his people, I'll bet some of his coun-
trymen would've still welcomed him back.
People are funny that way. Bet lot of us'd still
like to have Nixon back in the White House.
Look at what we got to follow him. Any better
ones? Like we used to say about a pretty girl:
"Any more like you at home?"

How about some more Babylon kind of
stuff, while I'm plunkin'? God was behind the
Israelites in killing off the Philistines. God is
always on the right side, even if that side is on
the left. I don't get the whole thing, but maybe
Ray and Lula can explain it to me some day.
The hardest part that I do get is that we got new
names to learn for places I never heard of. I just
begun to learn the names of all them Yugo-
slavic provinces, and up comes a new conflict.

In the meantime, I'll listen to all these
pundits engaging in retrospeak. Lula says I can
just turn it off if I don't like it. To me, it's all a
jumbled mess, and I listen to try to understand
it. I don't think she understands it, but pretends
like she does. Either that, or she's just able to
shut it off. Me, I wanna find out more and try to

understand. Probably never will.

The more I think about the troubles in the world, the more I think of how lucky I am to be born here. If there's a national pride we can endorse, it's probably wealth. With money you can buy anything, including the right to be the most powerful, and at the same time the most benevolent. Hey, Lula'd like me using that word.

Right now, we seem a little scared about what Iran's up to, like Ray having to go into seclusion right now, but I'll bet someone'll have it figured out pretty soon, using the almighty buck of course, and we'll simply be back to fighting our little campaign in Iraq and playing the stock market. Turning into a *big* campaign now though.

Sure glad I put some in, a few years back, when I did. How could I believe, when it was about six hundred or so, that it would be over ten thousand some day? That's the reason we can take this trip right now. It's the reason I could retire to Florida early, and Lula and me don't have to work right now. The good ol' U.S. of A. and its mighty dollar, that's why. At the same time we're killing some off in foreign lands in the name of God, we can go on TV and say it's for peace that we do it.

There's another highway sign now, just as I'm saying it. A billboard with an olive branch. The words, "Peace . . . give it a chance." in small letters. Almost too small for me to be able to read them from here. Better put on my prescriptions. If I get stopped, I'll probably have to be able to find where to sign on the dotted line.

Those kids in Wyoming were doers, not talkers. Just when we got smug, and thought you could figure a kid out by opening him up. The whole country was on a program. Some called it "Talk to a Kid". It was on the billboards too. Probably some still left.

Schools got all kinds of free money from the government, that's us of course, to invent programs for schools to talk with kids having problems. Then, when this latest stuff happens, they find out these kids left no note, didn't have a web page or diaries, two never even owned a gun, and everything we thought we had figured is just thrown out the window. Square one. The one that's still alive may not speak at all. He's still in a coma in Cheyenne. Only one school counselor knew one of the kids. Says he hated his parents and their lifestyle. I know I'm going on about this, but don't it bother everyone who knows about it? When we gonna be responsible about our brothers' actions?

Hell, me and Ray hated our parents lifestyle all the time we was growing up. Ever grow up in the middle of alkali trying to farm potatoes while the rest of the country's building shopping malls and water worlds for their kids? Many a time, I'd say to Ray, or he'd say to me after a hard day's work. "What're we gonna do now?"

"Shoot the folks," one of us'd say. Then

we'd sneak one of dad's beers to share so he wouldn't notice. There's a difference between talkin' and doing. One's protected by free speech, the other is only addressed in retro-speak by all them pundits.

CHAP 14. Introspection and plan

"What two books of the Bible have no mention of God?" I ask Lula.

"Wha . . .?" She comes up from her reading.

Then she says, "Books of Job and Esther . . . no, Esther and . . . Song of Solomon."

"Hmmm," I say, as she goes back to her reading. Course she's right. It's the only thing I remember being told in Sunday school.

We didn't have too much formal Bible learning back in Nevada. It wasn't the thing then. Isn't now, 'cept maybe for the fundamental churches that keep creeping in. Far's I know, that is. Where we grew up, the only close by church was Catholic. They don't follow the whole Bible too much from what I hear. Concentrated on the Gospels of the New Testament. Lots of Italians settled nearby. Catholic Church followed, or came first, for all I know. Went to the one in town a couple times. Went with Vince Pelligrini, one of the kids from school. His Dad was a potato farmer too. Some hay besides.

My ma was a Southern Baptist from Kentucky, but we'd a had to drive all the way to Winnemucca for church and that wasn't too easy, specially during the war years.

My dad was busy seven days a week besides, again mostly during the war. Besides what we owned, he leased some acreage and planted that too. Didn't even have a tractor till just when the war ended. By then he already had his sights on a cattle ranch over near Wild Horse. By then too, I was headed off to Elko for high school and that took up near all day by the time I got off the bus after dark. Ray went to a one room for two years before he joined me on the bus rides.

Shortly after that is when Ray trapped the wild horses for him and me, and before he got out of high school, my dad got kicked by one of our domestic bulls and that ended that.

I still have a lot of trouble talking about my pa. He was really a good guy, just acted like he wasn't sometimes. Hard making a living in a desert country with a wife and kids to support. Read a little about it in a book by some old-timer that drove all over the western landscape with a wife and family in a covered wagon near the turn of the last century.

As a widow, my ma didn't want to run a ranch all by herself, so she sold out and we moved down to Elko while Ray finished high school. By then I had made my first try at college, and near the end of the second year, decided that the University of Nevada-Reno wasn't for me. Oh, I took a few classes now and then as I thought about setting up a business in Reno. Mostly music classes so's I could get to appreciate my tuning and repair business a little better. It also helped get some new contacts for tuning jobs.

I got to know some of the faculty in the music department and eventually managed to get some accounts at the University. Sure was a help in getting me started.

I had gotten interested in piano tuning in the music store that I worked in part time and began tuning for some of the entertainment people at the clubs in Reno. Once in a while, they'd ship me down to Las Vegas to do a special assignment. That's after I got good. Finally opened up my own business after six years.

Ray had come over to Reno by then, and was a full-timer at the University. Majored in political history. Some teacher in Elko had got him started, and he won all kinds of awards and three local scholarships before coming over. One was for a speech he gave at the local Lion's contest. I forget the other two. He was a good student. Didn't matter what the subject was. He always had a fresh way of looking at something.

Like when he was a Senator from Nevada. He's making speeches in Congress. When the war in Kosovo is going on, he's making these speeches to support our troops, while at the same time chastising the leadership for not starting a new school for statesmen. For what? Nobody seemed to understand what he was talking about. A place where kids can go and learn how to get along with someone, with other countries and the like, he tried to explain.

He kept saying, that after the Revolutionary War and even during it, this country survived because we had people who were statesmen. Had the right stuff to know what to do in time of peace or war. He said, that over the years we lost that capability and somehow had to get it back. One way was to train people to become statespeople and serve the government in that capacity during times of crisis.

"For what?" they kept asking him. Somebody must've been listening though, cause now he's the Pres. We still ain't got a school for statesmen, but Ray has found enough people to work with and operate through him. Otherwise we would've had a much bigger scale action than we got going in Iran right now.

I think I know what it is. Those people over there have been fighting since the beginning, and I mean the beginning, of mankind according to the Bible, where mankind is supposed to have started. Iran is right nearby, so I know some of Noah's kids must've settled there.

That was after God's second take on humanity. Says he wasn't going to do it no more after that. Didn't either as far as I know.

If you read the Old Testament, you find that the place kept changing hands through warfare right up until recent times. Those people are used to fighting. Have a history of it. I guess so've we now, even if our country is a lot younger. They've got so little to start with over in that region of the world that they don't want to give up what they've got, easy like.

Course when all that oil wealth came in, they thought they was gonna be on easy street. And some of them was. Just the top dogs, though. You see pictures of the peoples' kids on TV and they've still got flies running in and out their noses like it's always been. No relief for the people. What they need is some new prophets, like in the Bible. Maybe *they* could use Ray's idea about a school for statesmen.

Lula's cell phone rings. "Yes," she says. "Lula Anne," she says.

I say, "Hang up." Someone's trying to zero in on our number. I read about it in a recent issue of AARP. She ignores me.

"Yes," she says. "Yes, —yes, —yes, —I understand, thank you." She hangs up.

I look over at her; my eyes make my arm swerve the car toward the next lane. From the look on her face, I restore my attention and get back in lane. An eighteen-wheeler toots me from behind.

"It's someone from the FBI. He's asking

about our destination."

"Why does he want to know that?" I say.

"Just in case they have to get in touch. Seems they need a neutral place for Ray and Maartha and the kids to hide."

"At the Ripples'? " I have this incredulous look on my face.

"They didn't say. Said they'd continue to be in touch. Says they'd appreciate it if we could get to our destination today. I told them yes, we could."

"Boy, I hope Jack and Alma have stored in a few extra cases," I joke.

"Why would the FBI want to hide the president in South Carolina?" she says.

"Hell if I know. Good idea though. Now at least we can get to see him for a while longer. You realize I ain't been alone with my own brother in a room where we can talk for more than a half hour in the last three years?"

"That's not all his fault," she says. I know what she's getting at. Maartha thinks we're on the downside, now that she's become First Lady. Wanted all our endorsements all while they're on the campaign trail. Come the election and it's all over. Lula really got pissed at her one time and told her so. Since then, we have trouble being in the same room together. Boy will she be pissed if she has to spend a week or something like that with us.

CHAP 15. End of interstate in sight

We're now driving in smelly rain. I forgot to wash the windshield when I filled up, and the collection of bugs along with worn wipers made such a mess, that I have to pull over and clean the windshield with a Wet One. It takes three sheets to do the whole plus the back window. On the road again, I contribute to the road smell with my wet shirt, hat and pants. A new cap, bought the prior weekend at the flea market, now ruined. I had paid a whole dollar for it. It was one of those pretty ones, with a couple of bluebirds imprinted. Bought one for Lula just like it, but she wouldn't wear hers. Says she'll give me hers when we get home. Better'n having a accident, she says of my cleaning the windshield. Should've waited like some of the other drivers I see, now stopped beneath a underpass. At least they're staying pretty dry.

A lot of the odor is coming from burnt rubber left on the road, but most is coming from the sawmills in this region putting out all that formaldehyde. At least that's what everyone says it is. I ain't no chemical man. Every time we drive through here, it smells the same if the wind's blowing right. I don't know how people living nearby can stand it. Get used to it I guess. Different places has different smells.

Like the cattle yards I remember. We didn't have too many in Nevada, but I remember going with my dad to Kansas one time to sell some of ours. Weee-ew! The smell was horrendous. Lula'd love that word too. Wet cattle probably even worse. Remember after a rare thunderstorm on the prairie, moseying among the cattle, listening to 'em lowin' on the hillside and smelling the aftereffects of their first bath in months.

Wipers seem to be working okay. Maybe just the cleaning was enough. I'll have to remember to buy some new Wet Ones before we get to Chapin. Remembered there's a shopping center about half hour before we get there. If we wait till Chapin, pay on the nose for what you can get in a discount store. Yeah, we'll stop before that.

Chapin is near where we're going on Lake Murray. It's just a little berg off the interstate on the old road to Greenville. Highway seventy-six if I remember right. Still have to drive about ten miles from there to Jack and Alma's place on the Lake.

Jacks folks bought the land on the lake back before the war. Put a house on it. Built it themselves.

He was my lieutenant in the service. Stationed in Texas together after I got drafted. He was in charge of special services on base, and when they looked up my records and found out I could tune pianos, he came and found me in my barracks. Wanted me to tune the piano in the base rec room. Got to talkin' and found him to be an excellent piano player.

We weren't supposed to fraternize on base, but he and Alma had a apartment off base and he'd invite me over on some weekends. He being from South Carolina, we didn't have too much in common, 'cept he always wanted to go out West and be a cowboy. So he wanted me to tell him all about where I grew up and some of the things I did as a kid; about horses and cows and the like. Course, sometimes, I'd embellish the stories I told, but he didn't seem to mind.

So after we got out of the service, he inherited this place on the lake that his folks had. His mother is in a nursing home nearby. To hear him tell it, his folks bought it for just a few dollars an acre after the Saluda Dam went up back in the early thirties. They bought the property at low water mark, and by the time the lake filled, they thought they was gonna have water coming into the living room. But it crested about twenty feet from the house and has stayed that way still.

Lots of other little towns and houses now under water along with some B-25 bombers from World War II. Heard Doolittle's crew used the lake for bomb-run practice there before the Tokyo raid. Even an island named *Bomb*. Can you believe it? Don't know if it's true or not. Lots of stuff springs up like that and after a while, people take it as facts. Maybe I can talk Lula Anne into doing some research on it. Better not. She'll want me to do it on my own after she teaches me a few more keystrokes on the computer.

Wants to buy a laptop now for when we travel. Without wires she says. Can get a signal anywhere there's a tower or something like it, she says. Can even write stuff on your phone now. I don't know about it. Can't keep up with everthin' that's going on now. Never could I guess. Learned one thing and stuck to it. Pianos'll always be around. Course there's electronic ones now too. Don't need much tuning there. But you ain't gonna see no concerts at Carnegie real soon on one of them. But it would be real handy I guess to have one at the Ripple's. Wouldn't have to wake them up early to get a password to use theirs. That's another thing about our sleep schedules when we're there, that I might tell you about later.

Lula and me really like to go there. They always give us the room that's facing the lake. When we look out in the morning, there's this small island with one tall tree that seems to be dead and petrified. It's got a eagles nest near the top and sometimes one inhabiting it. I take the binoculars and watch the eagle swoop down to catch some of the striper fingerlings in the lake. Sometimes a big one shows up in its paws. I guess I should say claws.

Now I look at the car clock and realize we're gonna have to push to get there before dark. "Does it matter?" Lula asks. Naw, I guess it don't. Don't know if I'll remember the way in the dark. There's a lot of turns before you get there.

Up above Beaufort somewhere, we take the turn off I-95 and head for Columbia. Now at least the scenery gets a little more interesting. People in the East talk about the boredom of the desert landscape. I'd sure like to know what's so interesting about the scenery along the eastern seaboard from South Carolina to the Keys. All looks the same to me.

So they come back with saying something about traveling through Utah from Salt Lake, then Nevada to Reno, as being the worse road they ever traveled.

Didn't you see the Great Salt Lake? I ask. What about Pilot Peak? Did you know about its historical significance to the pioneers? What about the Ruby Mountains, off in the distance, snow-capped, even in the summer just south of Elko? The hills of Battle Mountain; the welcome signs of Winnemucca. True, the Humboldt sink can be a little desolate. But did you see that special green color of the water at

Rye Patch?

What's I-95 got from here to the southern tip of Florida, I'm asking myself. A few rest stops here and there where you can get out, stretch a bit, and walk in some dog poop.

If Nevada's so great, how come you ain't living there, they always say. That's the Southern question to anyone espousing the beauty of where he comes from. All the snowbirds get the same treatment. So in recent times, I keep my mouth shut. Not gonna tell anyone about that secret wonder of the world, Lamoille Canyon, Nevada's answer to Yosemite.

"Need to make one stop at the liquor store," Lula says. I know right where she wants to go. Same as last time—a shopping center about a half hour this side of Chapin. Well, I was gonna stop for some new wipers anyway.

We get there, go in different directions, and I stretch while she makes a run for some gift wine. Don't know why. Jack and Alma are beer drinkers. Guess Lula wants some for herself. I look around. More beautiful hills paved over.

There should be a law that you have to put malls in a place nobody wants. How about a resurfaced disposal property? How about one atop of those garbage mountains in Florida? Some people say *dump*. Not me. I'm starting to gain on euphemisms. How ya like that one, Lula Anne?

CHAP 16. Help! The FBI has arrived!

We didn't know it, but while we were on the road, two men from a group of strangers is beating on the Ripple's front door. Two of them are back in a car, talking on the radio and looking around the property. They was Feds. That's the story we was told by the Ripples' later.

Were the feds ever surprised at what, or who greets them when they ring the doorbell. This Amazon-like woman answers the door saying, "Dem eenjy hebby he'lt."

Alma and Jack are saving her as a surprise to us. She's apparently a new girlfriend of their son Steve, and lives with him on a mountain near the North Carolina border. Suppose to be the highest point in the State of South Carolina.

All she gets is a blank stare from the lead officer. When he regroups, he asks, "The Ripple's residence, ma'am?"

"Lawd hab mussy! Lawd hab mussy!"

There's someone coming from behind the tall woman, though difficult to see. The agent steps aside, while his partner paws his weapon.

"Yes? May I help you?" Alma Ripple steps forward.

"Ma'am, do you have your television on?" the agent asks.

"Who are you?" says Alma.

"Ma'am, this is agent Kennedy (Kennedy nods), and I'm agent Stark with the FBI. It is our understanding that a Mr. and Mrs. Ed Galway are due to arrive at any moment. Is that true, ma'am, or have they arrived already?"

Alma never does think to ask for credentials, she's so surprised at the time. "No they're not here yet. Jack? Oh, Jack? Would you come here?" she calls into the room beyond the small hall entrance. Gullah-talking lady retreats into the house.

"May I ask who the lady is who received us ma'am?" agent Stark draws a notepad from an inside suit pocket. He borrows a pen from agent Kennedy.

"That's our . . . my son's friend."

"Is that some kind of code?"

"Code?" Alma asks.

"She sounds like some kind of jibberish talk, ma'am. Is that a signal to you for something?"

"I don't know much about FBI work, Mr. Stark, but no, that's not code. She speaks Gulluh at times when things seem queer."

"Gulluh, ma'am?"

"It's a language of the islands off the coast. You should hear my son speak it now, since they've . . . well, you don't want to hear of that."

"What is it mother?" Jack Ripple gets to the doorway.

"They say they're FBI, hon."

"May we come in sir?" agent Stark steps forward.

"Do you have some identification, officer?" Jack asks.

Agent Stark produces a wallet with a picture ID. "We shouldn't be long sir," he enters with agent Kennedy following.

"Your son home?" the agent looks around a large open interior accommodating several comfortable chairs, two tables, a television, a computer station, a fireplace and to one side, a full kitchen area set off by a floor-centered chopping table. It's appealing to look out from the inside of the Ripple's house.

With the curtains drawn, a full view of the lake extends from one edge of the room to the other. In the distance, the far shoreline appears at half-window length and in the background several small hills meet the skyline. Four small boats parade in the immediate view, and in the distance, an excursion vessel draws a barely visible wake. It's difficult from this distance to make out individual passengers.

"Steve? Oh no. He's on the mountain."

"The mountain?"

"Sassafras. Has a small cabin. Esther lives with him there," she looks toward the tall Mulatto who now stands by the fireplace, her hand adjusting pictures on one side while her dark eyes scrutinize Stark and Kennedy.

"Are you related to the . . . Kennedys'?" Alma asks the other agent, who until now had not said a word. She notes him eyeing the coconut bread, its cellophane wrap collecting condensation of fresh-bake.

"No ma'am, none at all."

"Would you gentlemen like coffee, and perhaps some coconut bread?" Alma asks, walking toward the kitchen area. When she gets to the kitchen window, she notes another man coming from the work shed about fifty yards from the house.

"Are there more of you?" she asks.

"Yes ma'am, two more."

"You haven't answered my question, Mr. and Mrs. Ripple. Have you been watching the news on television?"

"Yes, you mean about the president, don't you?" Alma says.

"Yes ma'am. We want to be sure the president's family is okay ma'am. Do you suppose you could give them a call?"

"You mean . . .?"

"No ma'am. He was on the road before we could call, and apparently has a new cell phone."

Alma and Jack look at one another. Both have similar thoughts: *The FBI without the ability to reach someone?* It seems confusing. Alma dials. In seconds Lula answers, and is informed of what has emerged in the last few minutes. Lula tells her they were coming anyway. She says she already talked with someone who says they were from the FBI.

"Yes," she turns to the agents, "they'll be here in about an hour."

"Mrs. Ripple, I'll be brief and direct, if I may," Stark says. "We're needing some place with reasonable security over the next few days, and the president mentioned yours as one that foreign powers would be most unlikely to know about. Do you get my meaning, ma'am?"

"You mean the president's coming here?" She turns and looks toward the fireplace. "Esther, you'll have to get the beds in the guest room re-sheeted. Call in Mathilda to help. My, I've got to go to the store, and do you think I'll have time to stop by Ella's salon and . . .? "

"Whoa, whoa, whoa, ma'am," Stark presses outstretched arms ahead of him. "No, Mrs. Ripple, I don't mean *you* have to entertain. That's not how we do things. I mean . . . we're going to take over your house for a short while. The president knows his brother is coming, so he'll want to visit. Do you possibly have a motel in town that our agents can accompany you to? Perhaps your son Steven's place on Sas . . . the mountain?" He thinks quickly about what he has just said, glances at Kennedy who returns an incredulous look, and corrects himself, "Scratch that."

"You mean you don't want us to be here? How are we going to entertain the president from a motel?" Alma's words sound desperate.

"I'm sorry ma'am, but in the middle of this kind of security that we're going to need, it is imperative that as few operatives as necessary are warranted."

"Set tuh de af' de boat," Esther vocalizes.

"What's that?" Stark questions.

Jack clarifies, "It means you're sort of treating us like second class."

"No sir, just protecting you and yours," Stark defers.

"De baa'b jook een 'e foot." Esther adds.

"I think I got that one," Kennedy speaks up. "It means . . ."

"Check the bedrooms," Stark cuts him off.

"Maybe we can go over to The Roses," Alma looks at Jack.

"You want me to go back to Steve's?" the Gulluh-speaking woman vocalizes in perfect English. Both agents' eyebrows lift.

"I'm sorry ma'am, but we'd like you to accompany the Ripples' at whatever motel they remain at."

He addresses both Jack and Alma again, this time with emphasis, "I'm sorry, but friends and neighbors won't do, folks. We've got to keep this simple. Look at it as a tax break. The

government is picking up the tab for the inconvenience.

"Now, may I have the cell phone number
of the president's brother? I'd like to speak with
him.

"No ma'am, don't write it down, just tell
me."

CHAP 17. FBI follow-Up

"What's a four-letter word for subversive?" I ask Lula as I start the crossword puzzle in the paper I got off the lawn before we left.

"Meek" she says. It's the right one. Both e's fit in the vertical columns. That's my Lula. Can't beat her in word contests. It's a gift. One I have to work at. I was never any good at Scrabble.

Funny, sometimes some big words just come to me out of the blue sky, if there's any sky in my thoughts, that is. That's the trouble I had when I started college after high school. Should've gone right into the business where I ended up. I can read a technical book and pretty much understand what it says. But if I take some poetry or fiction, I often find I'm rereading most of it cause I lost the point somewhere. Not Lula. She can remember the plot, characters, settings, everything. With me it's like reading the dictionary; no words tie together to make any sense.

Once read a story about a whooping crane. I think it was in grammar school. When I finished it, the teacher asked me what a crane was. I said it was one of them things you find on a construction site that lifts the ball and crams it into a wall to bring it down. Didn't have the slightest connection between the story and the bird. Got pretty embarrassed about it. Funny though, sometimes when I was working, some of my clientele—see, now I know what that is— used to have pretty good vocabularies. They'd be talking to me, and I'd pick up on a word or two that I didn't understand. Then I'd try to write it down soon's I got a chance so's I could look it up later to figure out what they was really saying.

That's another thing. I know sometimes I interchange *were* and *was* in the wrong place. It's an affectation that I learned growing up. Lots of Nevadans talk that way, or I should say, that-a-way. That's just the way we talk. Give us a chance to bet on it, and we can probably mix up "were" and "was" wrong ever' time. See that, I said "ever", instead of every.

I noticed a lot of people in Florida talked my way when I first got here. Must've had similar beginnings. Course the ones from New *Yourk* and New *Joisy* all think they speak correctly. The only ones to me that don't seem to have some sort of special language is native Californians. Maybe that's what we oughta do with our young 'uns—ship 'em all to Californie in their formative years, so's they can larn how to talk good. Maybe Arrrnold'll help. There I go, 'zaggeratin' again.

Anyhoo, in about fifteen minutes, we'll be at the Ripples' quarters, our temporary stay. I'm just thinking this and the phone is beeping. Can't figure who'd be calling, since we just bought the phone before we left, and only Jack and Alma know our number. So it must be them.

With Lula driving, I pick it up, "Hello?"

"Is this Mr. Galway?" someone asks. Oh no, not a solicitor already. How do those people do it? I'm about ready to say forget it, when the person continues, "Mr. Galway, this is agent Stark from the FBI, sir." He spells his name out. "We understand you are on your way to visit with the Ripples' in South Carolina?"

I'm about to ask if he can verify his identity by him telling me the color of my undershorts, but hey, what the hell.

"No, this is not the president of these United States," I say.

"We know that sir. We want to inform you that we are at your destination sir, and an agent will be meeting with you upon entry to the Chapin area. Would you please give us a description of your car sir, and the license number?"

"How do I know it's you?" I say.

"Who is it?" Lula asks. She's getting a little scared about my tone.

"Sir, is your social security number . . ." and he reads it off to me.

"Might be," I say. This is getting interesting to me now. I'm thinking of turning back home.

"Sir, someone we both know well will be arriving at the same destination as yourself shortly."

"You mean my aunt?" I fake.

"No sir, not your aunt."

"Mind telling me who then?" I say. Two can play this game.

"The person once owned a mottled gray horse," he says.

"What was the horse's name?" I say.

"Digger," he says back. I guess by now that he's legitimate, so I give him the information he wants.

"Thank you sir," he says. "Do you know about how far out you are time-wise?"

"About twenty minutes, I think."

"Fine sir, we'll be intercepting you shortly." Then he hangs up.

"What is it?" Lula pulls over at an off-ramp.

"The FBI. Apparently they've gone to Jack and Alma's and are waiting for us there now."

"What in the world for? Ed," she says.

"How would I know? Says that Ray is

gonna meet us there."

"I don't like the sound of this. Suppose we ought to stop and call the local FBI? What'd he say his name was?"

"Agent S-T-A-R-K, he spelled," I tell her. About then a helicopter buzzes overhead, makes a circle and comes back. I can see someone spotting us with binoculars.

"No sense in trying to turn around now," I say. "Whoever it is, they're on to us. Want me to drive?"

"No, I might as well finish. Besides, I'm not sure I remember the way in."

That's another thing. If I go somewhere, no matter how hard it is getting there, I can go back a year later and go right to the same place. Lula can go fifty times, and if she goes the following week, she can't find her way. Now does that make sense to anyone? Not to me.

So she crosses the intersecting road and gets back on the interstate still headed for Jack and Alma's. In five minutes we're at the exit for their place. After making several turns down some back roads, we get ready to turn at a fire station. When we do, a blue light flashes in Lula's rear view and she pulls over on a soft shoulder. "Not too far," I caution, "you'll get us stuck."

A guy gets out of and unmarked car, while another sits inside, with his ear pressed to a phone.

"Mrs. Galway?" he says to Lula.

"Yes sir," she says.

He identifies himself, I forget the name now, and wants us to turn around and go back to Chapin. She asks him why.

"We've made accommodations for you and the Ripples' in town ma'am," he says. "Just a temporary measure. Hope it won't inconvenience you both too much."

A euphemism for *"Tough shit buddy, and don't ask no more questions,"* is what he means. Another word for Lula.

When we get out of the ditch, we plaster mud all over the road and onto one side of the agent's car right behind us. I look around and see the windshield wipers diluting mud splatter. There is something good coming out of all this, I think to myself.

CHAP 18. The arrival

Although they don't have too much in common, there's one area that Lula and Maartha agree on: before leaving to go anywhere there's always some last minute thing each has to do.

At the last minute, before leaving Washington, Maartha wouldn't get on the helicopter before she took care of some exercise stuff she had on her computer. There was some kind of evaluation program that she had taught her "disciples" to use, one that monitored everything that had to do with an individual's exercise plan.

It told you how many pushups to do, for instance, then monitored your progress as to how you were doing with each one. Suppose you got to number four, and you didn't quite go all the way down or up, a little bell would ring and a voice would come on saying, "You were a little weak with that last interval sir," or ma'am, or whatever the case may be. Yep, now the whole country was gettin' in on part of computer evaluations during exercise.

She had a hard time convincing Ray to lend her name to the program at first. He was afraid the Democrats and Republicans would get a hold of it and use it to impeach him or something. Something about conflicts of interest or the like. Did I mention he was the first Independent candidate to be elected ever? Course it ain't always been Democratic and Republican like it is now. I looked it up in the Almanac.

They was Federalists, like President Washington; Democrat-Republicans, Whigs and the like. Didn't see no Independents though. Think the two parties we have now started back about Lincoln's time. Nope. Asked Lula about it later. Says it was Fremont, first Republican nominated, but he didn't win so I guess that don't count. The guy before Lincoln won and changed to a Democrat at the time. Martha's looking ahead to what the Independents'll bring after Ray leaves office.

Martha argued that it would be one of the fringes they would be able to cash in on after he got out of office. She likes that *famous* attention and all. Shoulda been a movie star. Think she did try out once. Saw some ex-senator or someone like that from the Congress doing it and thought it'd work for her too. But it didn't. Camera fright or something like that they called it. Not now. She sure got over it in a hurry with this new exercise routine.

Anyway, they didn't bother them about the exercise stuff. Not up front anyway. Course if you tuned in to C-Span, you'd always hear someone making a referral to "The First Lady's amendment to keeping America fit." Some reporter got it mixed up and wrote headlines, "The Lady's First Amendment to Keeping America Fit", and Maartha was on him like me on a carton of ice cream. Didn't want no one to think she was personally amending the constitution or some such. Did we hear about *that* for a while? Anyways, that was their expression for it. Then they'd chuckle about it and move on to something less serious.

So Maartha's got the whole FBI and CIA downloading her programs from the Internet, saving URLs, correspondence and any other thing related to her National Exercise Program.

Some, for the first time, learned how to use a search engine. One new FBI agent said facetiously that *Yahoo* was a Rebel yell for some kind of sexual innuendo between her and Ray. When he made the comment, two fellow agents hauled him off to another room and there was some loud talk going on.

So, while Ray and the girls wait in the helicopter, Maartha and six agents are still in the White House, gathering special computer stuff and any other equipment she can carry before coming out. She's planning ahead.

She says she wants to be able to broadcast from wherever they are soon as the coast is clear. Says she'll use the incident to attract more disciples, as she calls them. No one even has the guts to counsel her on the use of that word, "disciple". Someone thinks of turning it over to the yahoo who knows didley about *Yahoo*.

If it's left up to Ray, he'd a stayed back and waited for those Islamic perverts, or whoever those people were, and held them at bay from one of the White House windows with a .22 rifle. Hollow points at that.

He still likes to watch Sean Connery movies whenever he gets the chance. While he's a-waitin', he's having delusions. There's Connery, killing about forty guys with a handgun even though the opponents are armed to the teeth with assault rifles. This time, when the enemy tries to raid the fort, Ray'd be Connery and prevail. You shoulda knew him and me as kids.

I remember one time visiting some old historical bastion up in the Rubys; Fort Halleck, I think it was called. Nothing much there now. Ray got hold of some pictures of where the fort used to be, and when we thought we was at the right spot we moved a little higher up into the rocks nearby and began to shoot up the countryside with our rifles. We was there one afternoon, plinking off the rocks, whittling chips of volcano when this Boy Scout troop comes by. The leader yells at us, then comes up and chastises us for shooting so close to his little people.

"Hunting the new exotic partridges," we tell him. He calms down and tells us to be more careful. Never did ask why we'd be hunting birds with rifles.

***

So just about the time the helicopter is about to run out of fuel, out comes Maartha with three agents behind her carrying shopping bags and cardboard boxes full of disks and video cartridges.

"What's Momma gonna do with all that stuff, Daddy?" one of the girls asks.

"Lose three-eighths of a pound," he answers.

The other daughter shakes her head and goes back to her book. Then she looks up and says, "I'm gonna miss two finals, Pops." One of the agents aboard gives her a serious look. She notices, and adds, "POPS, do you think this will be over afore sundown? Those critters gotta get hungry sometime." Ray laughs at the way she's talkin'.

"That's enough, darlin'," Ray tells her. "This is a serious matter, and these gentlemen are doing all they can to protect our office."

The agent smirks at the daughter and leans back in his uncomfortable jump seat, adjusting the pads behind him for the third time.

"A stop at ampco avido," Maartha tells Ray. That's her idea of code. Old screwed up pig Latin. "I've got two cameras to pick up."

Ray nods at the pilot, and she'll have her way. The agents are already beginning to worry about their own lives and families'.

"Where are we ending up?" she asks one of the agents now seated beside her.

"We've got two units coming over from Fort Campbell, with the hundred and first," he says. "Preparations are being made for some-place in South Carolina, ma'am."

"South Carolina," she repeats. "Now what in hell would we . . . oh, no, not the Rip-ples' place," she says aloud.

"I'm not certain of the exact destination," the agent lies.

"Ray . . . RAY!" she yells above the roar of the helicopter blades. He pretends not to hear, instead, converses with his eldest. He's re-assuring her that she will be allowed to make up her work.

Maartha nudges the agent next to her and tells her to pass it along. In domino fashion, her words follow down the line, makes a u-turn to the other side and comes back to Ray. The agent sitting on his left cups a hand to Ray's ear. Ray looks over at Maartha.

"NOT THE RIPPLES' HOUSE!" her mouth exaggerates, her animations seen by all.

Ray opens his palms upward and gives his shoulders the heave-ho. Both daughters have gotten the message and Rayette, the older one, is now conversing with the younger about not having brought their swimsuits. She turns and complains to Ray. He tells her he's sure they'll be able to find one locally after they arrive. "But, we won't be outside too much, I don't think," he adds. Now they're starting to pin him down on the length of stay.

It's getting near dark, and the 'copter is headed up into the Blue Ridge toward West Virginia. There's a headquarters there that they'll stop at to make the transfer to two more whirlybirds. The stop at Camp David takes only twenty minutes, a new record for Maartha.

"Watch her on TV," Ray says to everyone in hearing distance. "She packs more routines in thirty minutes of exercise than any video on the market. But trying to follow her after she gets off the tube is like trying to dig your way through a granite mountain with her running the drills."

He's always given to a little hyperbole when it comes to Maartha. But I guess it's true of some. I'm lucky that-a-way. Lula's a wham-bammer. She likes to get it all done quick-like so's she can get on with her leisure, she says.

It's near midnight when the whole bunch ends up near Chapin at a local rec center that has a couple of ball fields where the helicopters can land. Some cars are waiting, and the Ray ensemble is all whisked away in a few minutes, headed toward the lake. The local population don't hear a word about it. An overnight patrol at the rec center is offered a bribe from the agents, after being told that a local National Guard mission is underway, coordinating activities with the current situation in Iran. They act like they understand, and refuse to take any reward for their silence.

"Glad to do our duty," the officer in charge tells the agents.

CHAP 19. Carolina in the morning

Next morning, Maartha is ready to do her thing. This is what I find out about while me and the wife is in temporary storage.

Two agents and the president prepare for a little nearby roadwork as Maartha and two assistants begin setting up. Cameras are readied to tape and later broadcast a syndicated program to her "disciples" on early morning TV.

It's going have to be taped, since the undisclosed location can't be accessed in view of the present crisis. Immediately, she begins to investigate resources in the room to incorporate activities into her routine. She's operated this way from the beginning. "Give the public variety, show interest in what you are doing, and they will participate," becomes one more slogan.

With dawn approaching, she utilizes the Ripples' broad living room for her background. Seen in the backdrop, through floor-to-ceiling glass panes, the lake appears serene, etched in patches of morning fog.

From the living room wall, Maartha grasps a military sword that she's eyed on the previous evening, a Samurai, and begins to undulate, drawing the instrument in its scabbard between her thighs, up, over her head and behind. As her arm shifts backwards, she transfers the grip to her opposite hand and continues the movement forward to its original position. All the while, her sophomoric, affected voice, directs her disciples to do likewise with whatever stuff they can find convenient in the proximity of their own kitchens, parlors, and dens. "A one, and a two . . ." she continues with words borrowed from music guru Welk.

In thirty minutes, the tape completed, she dines at breakfast with consort agents awaiting the president's return from his morning jog-a-thon.

As she eats from a repast of her own design, she flips pages of a local publication that describes the lake and its environs from earliest creation. One article dominates her perusal, a subject she eagerly anticipates discussing with her husband upon his return. She can barely wait until he finishes showering, then joining her at breakfast. When he's seated himself opposite her on the screened porch at a large oak table, she neglects the usual morning greeting, and cuts to the subject.

"Do you know there's about thirty B-25's on the bottom of this lake?" Maartha says.

"Nope, and we don't need 'em," answers the president. "Trying to concentrate on those Apaches, besides."

"I know we don't need them darling," she continues, "but what an excellent exercise routine it would make!"

The president looks up, ponders briefly, lets the words swirl for a bit in the convolutions of gray matter, and then returns to yesterday's copy of the Wall Street Journal.

"You know, I could make a tape of increasing one's lung capacity by going diving for artifacts that are part of our nation's history."

"You mean with a snorkel?" he says.

"A snorkel, tanks, whatever. The point is to be able to hold one's breath for a long period of time, not in an artificial way, but the real thing."

"Go for it," the president agrees. "Only today, we still gotta lay low. Takes practice Martha. Had a lot of experience with it. Ever trap wild horses? Takes patience. Waiting for news on our next move. Hoping to see Ed and Lula, besides. I don't think it'd be good to get out there today. What about you going shopping with the girls? I think we can find some disguises so's people around Columbia won't recognize."

"The girls wanted to sleep in," Maartha

pouts. "You know what that means."

"Yeah, they won't be up for breakfast or lunch."

"Right, darlin'. In the meantime, do you suppose I could go out on the Ripples' boat and survey the area for a possible dive at some later date?"

"Don't suppose it would hurt. Take Henry and that Kennedy fella with you. And if we say get in here fast, just do it, okay?"

"Fine, darlin' I'll get my suit," she bubbles, leaving the table after swiftly kissing her husband on the cheek, as she brushes past.

In the Ripples' living room, agents and aides play a rerun of the morning's taped session. As Maartha strides past, gratuitous remarks replace their earlier conversation evaluating her performance.

"Glad you like it," she continues, entering the hall, making her way to the master bedroom where an assistant is waiting to attend to her bath and dressing.

With nothing else to do, the living room crew reviews another tape from one of the boxes, archives that have been taken from the White House.

In episode forty-two, Maartha describes a hoop, its structure much like a classic Hula Hoop from which a section had been removed. When twirled at the waist, the hoop is released at the opening and when ready, caught mid-air. The objective is to improve reaction time and coordination.

In another episode, a scene depicts Maartha in a wintry Vermont setting, this time in full leather, standing beside a naked staff, a debarked birch tree, topped at about eight feet. After brief instructions, Maartha shimmies the birch, using matching leather gloves, and grasps the trunk with both hands about two inches from the apex. Then she begins to slowly press her weight to one side, allowing the birch to recover on its own accord, bringing her back upright, then past her initial position to the opposite side, simulating a giant metronome. All the while, she explains the importance of maintaining one's balance in recovery; an added feature of exercising muscles that one seldom uses.

"Why do it?" an agent blurts, an outburst he regrets immediately.

"Shush!" come several responses, with heads turning to see if he has been overheard. At the porch breakfast table, the president pretends not to hear; his attention returns to a column on the next page.

Shortly after the tape was released, a Vermont environmentalist group decries its marketing, stating fears that mountains of Vermont birches, in an orgy of winter exercise, would hasten to quick deaths as the populace ascends hills to emulate their leader. Not to fear. Not Vermonters.

When interviewed by a reporter, Max Crescent, a local native, expresses frankness about the whole affair: "Looks like a bunch of penises out there. With no heads," he adds. "I don't think the First Lady should be bending a bunch of penises like that in front of the whole country. Save it for the bedroom. What's she thinking, anyways?"

"Yes, sir, thank you," the reporter yanks the microphone out of voice range. "Well, you've heard it from one of the locals," the reporter says. "Now back to studios in Atlanta."

The scene changes to CNN studios where two news anchors are caught cracking up and recomposing themselves.

CHAP 20. The new war rooms

Again as we find out later, while we're all getting organized for defensive purposes, here's what's happened with the terror situation:

Commander Lasting and crew are now in open water over the Atlantic Ridge. In the abyss below, fissures on the ocean floor are still adding molten earth to that already solidified over the millennia, creating new crust, spreading floor surface to eventually become dry land at coastal margins. This has been going on since the beginning of earth time.

A check on sub radar reveals nothing in the vicinity, as Lasting surveys the horizon from the bridge, his vision filtered by a warm sea breeze. He feels ecstatic to be back in command again. If only circumstances were different. Too late for regrets.

From a satellite relay, a voice on his cell phone tells him exactly what he deems practical. His funds safely deposited. Beyond reach of inquiry. He dials a backup number and again receives assurance. Another call tells him his escape route is also confirmed. In an hour he's below deck and below horizon, informing his crew about individual concerns.

"We have been guaranteed by our sponsor that rescue has been plotted at the exact lat and lon," he addressed them. "Good luck to all." The cause justified. "See you all at Cannes."

Every selected member in accord. All except one: a *Judas* aboard. Lasting couldn't know, even beyond extensive initial screening, that of which he had been reassured.

He orders a speed increase to 23 knots, near maximum for this sub. The Typhoon class sub strains against its front horizontal hydroplanes as sounds are muffled in reflection from absorbing tiles on interior panels.

Although capable of carrying twenty ballistic missiles, only ten have been acquired by launch date. It would be sufficient. During the next morning, his crew practices escape from two chambers housed on either side of the sail. In afternoons they engage in simulated practice of all missile systems.

Not since the nineteenth century has the Capitol felt the sting of a foreign bee. The plan:

Six missiles for Washington, the remainder for selected alter-thrones. Cripple shots only. Not intended for national destruction. Each missile retrofitted with conventional warheads, a similar kind as those used in the desert on a retreating people, in place of the original one hundred kiloton nuclear design. Retribution at hand, at the hand of an alienated submarine commander with an equally alienated crew, except for one.

At his desk, Commander Lasting reviews a report he has scrutinized on several occasions. An important caution, it tells of the accident that had occurred with the R-39U missile in an explosion shortly after launch in November of 1997. There had been severe damage to the submarine's infrastructure. A faulty booster had been thought to be the cause. All systems involving boosters would receive double checks; triple if necessary. Any malfunctions would scratch the offending missiles, possibly aborting the mission.

In the engine room, twin nuclear water reactors transmit energy through mechanical couplings to the fixed seven-blade propellers. Lasting is counting on them to remain operational throughout the mission, obviating need of use of supplemental 800 kW diesels.

Beneath the torpedo room, its tubes empty, a sonar operates continuously. Lasting has rejected an offer at last minute before launch to fit the vessel with torpedoes. Time was of the essence. In an announcement to the

crew, he emphasizes the mission to be of
blitzkreig proportions, using a term borrowed
from World War Two. Besides radar, surface
buoys interface with satellite communication
systems designed to maximize full interaction.

The new gymnasium, solarium and
swimming pool have been retrofit with substitute equipment; a supply consisting of scuba
gear, inflatable rafts, sails, non-perishable
foods, fishing equipment and electronic communication gear.

A sauna, a luxury item, was the least of
necessities for the short mission. Intended to
enhance habitability, adjacent rooms had been
designed to harbor several domestic species of
birds and small mammals, an art gallery, chef's
stand, a bar, and pool tables.

One of four of the original six subs to be
deactivated during 1998, this submarine had
been purchased by Iran prior to formation of
U.S. Senator Lugar's monitoring committee.
Subsequent dismantling of all Typhoons was
slated for 1999. In a failing economy, Russia
sought funds from external sources. With the
coming of the Iran insurrection, the purchase
and retrofit were haphazardly monitored by al-
lied countries.

Even though the movement of the sub
appeared harmless, seemingly intent on being
housed by its purchaser at a base in the Persian
Gulf, its departure and possible threat of hostil-
ity between principals was hardly investigated
by U.S. intelligence. When it suddenly veered

from its expected route just past the Azores, some officials at Congress became concerned. Not all.

"A shakedown run", several Congressmen assured TV pundits on "Meet the Press". It would turn, they said, and eventually continue on its intended path, a home base somewhere in the Middle East.

Only in the last few days had it become clear, that despite monitoring the zigzag path, it appeared the sub's new destination was off waters near Cuba. Officials rendered a yellow light to the White House and Pentagon.

"Remove to Nevada?" a CIA official spoke with the president.

"In the middle of the week?" the president responded.

"I see your point, sir. A trip to Camp David perhaps?" the counter-offer.

"It's a vacation retreat."

"What do you suggest, sir?"

"A meeting with my brother. He's traveling through South Carolina to be with friends before he comes here. Let's call it a death in the family, but don't disclose the location. Want to keep it private, let's say."

"Fine sir, might work. Don't worry sir, whatever they're up to, we won't let it happen."

"Hmmm," the president countered, "better not. There's a lot of people gonna die needlessly on both sides if it does, whatever it is."

"Yes sir. We'll soon have full monitoring

sir. Our field agents say they're on top of the whole thing."

"Sure they are. In the meantime, can we get some information to some freshman Congressman to inquire about what happened to the supposed four hundred million that Lugar is supposed to have promised for the dismantling, but the Russians claim they never agreed to? We've got to create a diversion. Get the news media off it, just in case it happens. Course if it does, all the discussion on the floor will have been for naught, right?"

"Sir, I'm not sure if . . .?"

"It's nuclear, right?"

"Yes sir."

"Our sources?"

"They don't think so, sir. Think it's been retrofitted."

"Let's hope so. But in the meantime, let's get our priorities focused. Let's keep on the horn to Moscow; also our embassies in Pakistan and Iran."

"Right, sir.

"Will you be having lunch here, sir?"

"Get me on the horn to Ed. What motel did you say he was at?"

CHAP 21. Bible study group

In a suite of rooms at The Roses motel in Chapin, hardly anyone passes the night in fruitful sleep. Jack and Alma share a room, as do us Galways. Esther has her own room and two FBI agents take the last.

For spending overnight, agent Ross warns us about not leaving rooms. In an emergency, we can dial his number. He tells us that all calls to any outside line are gonna be routed through him. He takes all our cell phones away saying, "Just a precaution until we know better about tomorrow."

With everyone settled into respective rooms following an exhaustive day of movement and political intrigue, the FBI agents place sticky marking tape at the intersection of doors and frames of each of the rooms occupied by us. We're all warned again, not to leave without calling first. So us *clients* spend the night in isolation from one another and from the outside environment.

Agent Stark says he hopes the crisis will be over before locals can get wind of our movements. He makes it known to all that playing a role in this secrecy is important, especially for the President. He asks that we cooperate in the name of Homeland Security. He invokes mother, God, and all the rest. He misses apple pie.

We assure him of our willingness to cooperate, but in turn, ask for regular drink and meals on time. He tells us that's gonna be the easy part. He has a plan as to how to move us about without their being noticed as individuals. One of the oldest deceptions in human endeavor, he says. I can't wait to know.

***

The agents, sandwiched between two adjacent rooms housing us clients, are awakened in pre-dawn hour by a series of rumblings and slamming of doors and water running in bathrooms.

"Might as well do it," one turns to the other, kicking back blankets, contorting himself in early morning exercise while still prone in bed.

***

"Everyone ready for breakfast?" agent

Stark knocks on our doors after removing security tape. Bet that looked interesting to other
guests staying here.

In about an hour, the Ripples, us and
Esther are loaded into a white panel Ford van
with two agents. Agent Stark takes a white
magnetic placard with black lettering and posts
it on an exterior side panel. It reads MEDIAN
BIBLE CHURCH. The other agent, Ross, pilots
the vehicle along back roads until we reach old
Highway 76. In a nearby town, the van stops at
a Burger King.

"This okay with everyone?" Stark asks.

"Couldn't we go on farther into Columbia
and eat at a . . . *different* place?" Alma says.

"Ma'am, we know this may not be your
style of dining and all," Stark answers, "but
we've got to appear to be what the sign on the
outside of this van says."

Makes sense to me, I think. Here we are,
five white people, one black agent and one mulatto woman, on our way to a Bible convention
somewhere. No time for silver service. We des-
ignate the black agent as our preacher. He don't
smile about it.

"Will we have time to drop out to the
place to visit with Ray soon?" I ask, while waiting for my ninety-nine cent's special: egg,
sausage and cheese croissant.

"I'll inquire sir, after everyone's seated."

Yeah, that won't look suspicious at all.
Everyone sittin' around two tables, slung together, while one guy is on a cell phone. Even

in Chapin it's hard to hide with a black pin-
stripe suit on. In a few minutes, the answer
comes. No, it won't be possible right now. We
can stop by a local Wal-Mart on the way back
and buy some games to play if we want.

After breakfast, we do just that. He tells
us before we go in we're to stay together, talk in
lovin' terms and all. Be polite to each other. Act
like real church-types. He's a lecturer, I can tell.

While we're in Wal-Mart, the agent's
phone beeps. It's Ray, and he wants to talk to
me.

He's all-apologetic about not coming to
see us at the motel. He knows it's inconvenient
for everyone, and apologizes all over the place,
all the while addressing me as "Moose", my
childhood nickname. I might tell you about that
later. He says he's still hoping to perform on
Sunday evening, and hopes we're all still interested. *Me and Maartha* is the way he puts it.

I ask if we can bring along Jack, Alma,
Esther and Steve. Maybe a agent or two that I
say I've been friendly with.

He understands right away that I'm just
joshing and ignores my request. Just the *names
on the invite*, he says; just like that. He uses the
words just like that. Like he knows how I'd use
it. That Ray. Didn't I say how he had this silver
tongue? He says everything should be cleared
up by then.

When we all leave Wal-Mart, we've got
packages that include Scrabble, three electronic
Bass Fishermen games, six sets of dice, and

four decks of playing cards. In addition, to make us look authentic, Alma has purchased two Bibles, telling the clerk at checkout, that she doesn't want them bagged.

The mid-week Sunday school bunch is on its way again. Alma begins a chorus of "The Old Rugged Cross" as we get back on Highway 76. Everyone except the two agents join in. Stark raises his eyebrows at Ross, the driver, who's looking back at him in the rear view mirror.

One of the agents has picked up assorted snacks for all, so's we won't have to find an excuse to leave our rooms. This is gonna be fun, I'm thinking. Solitary, for an undetermined length. No trial, neither. I look around and figure we all might be able to handle it better'n the agents.

"Mucker anyone?" Alma says after we get resettled back in the motel compound. No trial neither. She tears open two packages of dice. We need six, and they're packaged in fives. She tosses four into the bottom of a Wal-Mart plastic bag. From the bathroom sink she opens a packaged plastic cup to use as a die shaker.

Esther don't want to play. Says she's gonna spend some time with her new Bible.

"Uh glad fuh hab dey cump'ny," she says. She's not even nervous this time. Alma and Jack have a big laugh over it. Stark stares ahead, not wanting to join in, but I can see he's straining.

"She's nervous again," Alma faux whispers to all gathered at the table.

We all roll for first shake and Jack wins. On his very first roll he gets a "wheel" and a thousand points. On his next required roll, he gets one five, and stops with a total of one thousand and fifty. He passes the six dies to me.

Both agents sit in front of the TV on one side of the room, tuned to CNN.

Reporters are still telling of the president being at Camp David, working on a important strategy toward ending the Iranian crisis. Only one reporter is still on the tail of a story from a important White House source that says something about the imminent danger to Washington posed by a foreign power. His thoughts are largely discounted by most of the media.

***

In a New York apartment, a message translated by a rabbinical scholar has arrived. A submarine is in position at maximum depth off the waters of the Bahamas. The code translation is relayed instantaneously to the Pentagon and operations are put into motion for a major deployment and interception.

Another mole has been in touch since Lasting's departure from Idaho. One of Lasting's poker buddies has been monitoring his activity for Homeland Security after he arrived in his relocation.

At FBI headquarters, profiles of Commander Lasting and several co-conspirators fill computer screens. Detailed files are selected and stored in desktop folders. The threat is interpreted as real and imminent. The poker buddy, a spy working for U.S. security in Idaho, remains in contact continuously. The mole gives additional details about sub-plots that have happened in the past few weeks before Lasting's departure. Spies everywhere.

***

"Whatcha readin' now?" I ask Esther.

"De Lawd cyas' Mistuh Adam en' Miss Ebe out de gyaa'd'n," she says.

"You haven't gotten very far," I quip. No one seems to be paying attention to our conversation, mostly glued to news reports and staring into empty space by now.

"No, I haven't, Mr. Galway," Esther says. "Actually, I've been thinking that when this is all over, I'll be glad to get back to Steven and some semblance of normality in preferred isolation."

She's calm again.

"Like it up there on the mountain, I take it."

"Most consoling," she says. "I know his parents need the assistance and we can use the extra shekels, but this experience has been most unnerving. Not only that, but he's expecting to have heard from me by now."

"I don't know where this is all going, Esther, but I'm sort of in agreement with you. Sometimes this world gets a little complicated for even me, and I'm not that complicated a thinker."

We share a communal smile with those
who have tuned into our conversation.

CHAP 22. A little more about me; you know, the president's brother

We're already tired of the games. To pass my own time away in this seclusion, I begin to think about my past career as a piano tuner.

I look around the "suite", a regular motel room with the adjoining doors, half unlocked. Everyone else seems to be doing the same. They're staring at the TV with glazed expressions. Agents run in and out of the room with fresh coffee, but no one seems to notice them anymore. It's like they are part of the *invited* group. And we've all become part of the furniture.

I think about the time just after I started with my own business in Reno. I had received just enough accolades from the circuit performers at the clubs to encourage me to open a studio on a back street downtown. I've heard they've torn it up since, making way for new development. One springtime flood from the Truckee was all it took to encourage some re-routing of the downtown area.

One of the performers, who I'll allow to remain nameless, provided a lot of the backing I started with.

By then, my mother was living with us, me and a new wife, in Reno; Ray had gone on to bigger and better things, with a wife and a budding career, as a public defendant. Now he was running for Congressional leadership from our district. In the next election he made it to Washington.

Don't know if I mentioned, but that marriage was his first. Her name was Kathleen, a singer with one of the bands that routinely came through the clubs. Her bandleader was the one who backed me. She got killed on the grade above Carson City about ten years after they married. Maartha is his second wife, much younger than Ray, thus accounting for two kids in college right now.

Anyway, I had contracted with the University to do all their pianos on a rotating basis. It turned out to be a bread and butter deal. With the regular business fluctuating a lot, including time for travel, regular activity at the music department provided income I could bank on. Course, Lula's teaching salary didn't hurt at the time either.

About two months into my tuning I had made a couple of rounds of the studio including teacher's and student's pianos. I'd taken a few actions back to the shop for minor repairs and the like.

One morning, the department head calls me into his office. "How's it going?" he says.

"Just fine. Good work and a pleasant faculty," I answer.

"Had a little problem," he offers.

I wait.

"Two of the instructors seem to be having difficulty with some tunings. They've mentioned it to me a couple times. Wonder if you could check their pianos over a bit."

Right away, I know who he's talkin' about. Two profs, both about the same age, one a violin teacher, the other a voice teacher, never did give me the time of day from the start. Seems one of them's husbands had been the tuner-technician for a number of years. They sung his praises ever chance they got. When he passed away, the department waited for about a year then gave me a chance based on the recommendation of my own benefactor. Well, I'm this young upstart who's going to come in and take over from the master. I think you get the picture. I could've been Job and that wouldn't have mattered a salt pillar.

So I went back and gave them special treatment. It didn't matter. Still complained. Besides that, their opinions carried a lot of weight with the chairman. I thought sure my contract would not be renewed the following spring. So I just did the best I could, talked it over with the missus, and awaited my fate. In the meantime, I use my own version of the ratchet system to secure more accounts. One was to make the rounds of some of the clubs opening in the Tahoe area.

After Christmas that year, a number of concerts were scheduled in the campus auditorium. The Chairman asked me if I was willing to fine-tune the grand prior to the concerts, or should he get some outside help?

No, I told him. Under our contract, it was agreed that I was to provide tuning and maintenance for all campus pianos, including the performance grands. He agreed and let it go at that.

Well, I spent some extra days on the weekend on campus, and some extra time on the same evening prior to the concert. I felt sure that my tuning was correct. I had a feeling I knew why the little ladies complained, and it wasn't all because of Job.

I had been using a non-traditional style temperament. A temperament is sort of like a standard, using one set of twelve tones around the middle of the keyboard, then everything builds from there in both directions until all eighty-eight are in tune. About ninety percent of tuners use the same temperament. I'm one of the other ten percent. It came from the way I tried after reading a book that was put together by a physicist and piano technician, in which it explained a much simpler tuning method. Not only that, but the added benefit was that it resulted in the treble tones coming out brighter, the way that singers and orchestra leaders really like. I had always gotten some pretty good compliments from those two groups.

So this famous concert pianist comes to town. I won't name her, but she's right up there with Claudio Arrau and Andre Watts. She comes in, does her concert, and leaves. Everyone is talking about her great performance, except the two ladies. They're not badmouthing me about the tuning, however. They've been told, I hear later, that someone was brought in from the outside to do the job. They're both cautious at first about saying anything, and both me and the department chairman are keeping our distance from them.

About a week later, at about the same time, I hear they've been talking about the improved tuning, cause they think someone else done it.

Then I see a letter on the bulletin board outside the main office. Not only one, but two copies are posted on the same board. It's from the pianist who performed the week before. In it, she says she's especially thankful for the fine-tuning of the piano that she used. She hasn't played with such bright tones anywhere in the West quite like it. The last time was on the stage at Carnegie. Just about the time I finish the letter, the chairman peeps around the door

to the office and gives me a wink. I know he's
told them who actually tuned. I smile but re-
frain from gloating, though I really want to.
Needless to mention, the following spring, my
contract is renewed for another two years. The
little ladies never say another word about my
tuning, and I don't bother to ask again if everything's okay.

CHAP 23. Hideout adjustments

At the Ripples' place, Maartha is taping her morning session away from home. It was supposed to be taped on the commons, using the Washington monument as a backdrop. Assorted branches trimmed from cherry trees were to be used as props for her morning routine.

Instead, after daylight and a quick Cappuccino, she scrounges the outside shed and brings back two disassembled leaf springs that's been removed from an old car that Jack had restored, and then wrecked. In the front yard, at water's edge she begins to gyrate a leaf in both hands, its undulations transmitting vibrations to her flesh, that ripples sympathetically in damping amplitude of the spring energy. I know about that amplitude and energy stuff. Same kind we use in piano work.

"Let's program this one," she directs an assistant who aims a personal camera at the First Lady.

After a series of repetitive movements, the assistant tells her she has collected enough data to feed to an online computer. When an uploaded screen appears on the monitor, a connection is made between the camera and the viewed program. Numerous dots that simulate movements of a single cycle in Maartha's workout begin to appear on the screen.

From a view option, the assistant selects "trace" and lines connecting the dots appear. Two more keystrokes and the number of calories burned per repetition appear in a totals column. From there, any number of selections can be made, designed to monitor a complete workout with the use of the new device. At the end of a workout, the program congratulates the user both with vocal and written message. Another calculation automatically begins to take shape in instructional planning for the next workout.

Maartha loves her new toy. In the works are patent rights on a new computer program, as an offshoot to an original she has used for the past three years. Marketing will begin when her husband leaves office.

Maartha isn't the only one who's managed to take some personals with her on this hiatus. The first thing Ray grabbed was his hand-made guitar. It's a prototype, I forget the

name, assembled by a colleague after much sci-
entific research in the seventies. That's when
guitar was big. For the first time in the history
of the United States, kids wanted to grow up to
be guitar players. No doubt, Elvis and the
Beatles had a lot to do with it.

Ray started way before its populariza-
tion, in Mexico, where he had gotten a
scholarship for study. While there, he noted
how popular both the guitar and bullfighting
was among the nation's people. So part time, he
took up the study of guitar and began to devote
long periods to daily practice. He never did take
to cavorting with his fellow students nights and
weekends. Probably, because of being in tune
with himself, as any desert flower might be.
Heck, you grow up with nothing but cactus and
sage to look at in your formative years and it's
hard for shopping malls and loose women to
tempt you. Scratch the latter. Ray and me did
do our share of fraternizing in Reno and Elko in
the early days.

But in Mexico, he stuck with it. Practicing Segovia's major and minor diatonic scales.
Then special legatos, difficult passages, and
new pieces. Within a year, he was sufficiently
practiced to play three minor pieces by mem-
ory. You'd think a person starting this late
would have given up. Not Ray. Remember,
when I started all this talk, I told you how he
never gave up on anything.

When he got back to Nevada, he found
the best guitar player he could, and after several

trials, took on a teacher while he was finishing his graduate work. Hell, he was so devoted, sometimes he wouldn't even show up for the annual Fourth of July celebration in Jarbidge.

"Got to give a concert at the local library," he once said, as a excuse. The local library? He was good enough for that already?

When he started practicing law, about seven years later, he posted some billboards around Sparks. There was a picture of him, and the caption told of a coming solo performance at the high school auditorium. "I thought you was a lawyer," some'd say. "I am," he'd answer, and hand an admirer his card.

So now he's at the Ripples' home, in one of their bedrooms, a practicing away with the doors and windows shutting away the distractions.

Maartha's in the living room reviewing her takes, laughing and flirting with the agents, who are telling her how much they appreciate the influence she's having on our nation's youth, particularly the young women. She's eating it all up. Wants to know all about the shotguns they carry, while in the back of her mind, trying to figure out how she can work it into a new routine. Maybe tape it by the end of the week.

Outside, antennas are being set up to be able to receive info directly via satellite from Washington, West Virginia and New York.

Noise all around, and Ray is going through selections for his performance on Sunday evening. Best thing that has happened to him right now the way he sees it. He wouldn't have had nearly enough time for practice if he'd a been back in the White House. Maybe the critics would lighten up this time. He was already sorry he'd been talked into it. He read somewhere that Segovia practiced for almost a year on a piece before performing it in public. This time, Ray is adding two new pieces after six months of practice. Not smart. No Segovia is he.

A rap on the door.

"What is it?" Ray sighs, looks up at the inside oak-varnished woodwork.

"May I come in, briefly, sir?" Kennedy says through the door.

Ray lets him in.

"Sorry to disturb you sir, but we've had news. A submarine has been detected off the Bahamas, between the Bahamas and Cuba."

"Castro involved?"

"We're not sure, Sir. That's what we're trying to intercept now."

"Hostile?" Ray asks.

The agent raises his brow.

"Okay, what does the Pentagon say?"

"They're sending in sub chasers and are going to try to communicate."

"Just a practice run?" Ray asks.

"Not according to interceptions we've made in New York and Miami. Right now we're forcing communication from two raid points on the inside. Iranian nationals. They've decided to cooperate. Never wanted in on their instructions in the first place. They came, they saw and liked what was already here."

"Okay, keep me up," Ray says, dismisses Kennedy, and goes back to practicing some tremolos.

***

I'm in the motel room after lunch trying to dial Ray at the Ripples' place, but they've got it all tied up with busy signals. They've forgotten Jack and Alma have another line, and son Steve gets through. The agent is about to reach for her phone and remind her about the agreed to warning, but Jack stares him down. Even at his age, I think Jack could've give the agent quite a tussle.

"Make it short," Jack says to Alma.

Steve's askin' about Esther. Should've been back on Sassafras by now. But the agent has another trick. Twice Steve's told he has the wrong number and gets a busy signal from then on.

"Damn," Alma looks at Stark, "take the block off."

"Sorry ma'am," Stark says.

Steve calls friends nearby, and they say they'll check on it for him.

CHAP 24. Intrigue

Son Steve's no dummy. He's a dropout from the Vietnam era. Had enough with all that repatriation stuff, and decided to take his disability and live on a mountain in South Carolina. It's a place he's gone to camp on vacation since he was a kid.

During the conflict, his folks bought some land on the slope and give it to him as a welcome home present. His Dad is proud of him for serving, as we all are. Another war, like the one we were in, that no one in Washington declared. So we've sort of got that in common with Steve.

Steve's job is in electronics while in the service, communications specialist of some sort, so when he's out, he naturally gravitates to computers. He's taken a couple years at Clemson, but don't finish his degree. So now he moves up to the mountains with his girlfriend, a Gullah woman from the islands off the coast, and they set up housekeeping in a cabin. While he plays with the Internet, she's writing stories and cleaning and organizing Jack and Alma's house.

Course, Lula just finds that out on our current outing, that Esther writes, and now the two are inseparable. The writing stuff, that is. They talk about maybe collaborating on writing some children's stories together.

Esther and Steve ain't married, or at least haven't admitted to it. Jack and Alma are having trouble with the racial thing at first, but Esther's intellectual distractions take effect and they've begun to take her in as one of their own.

Steve's got a gifted side. With the help of the Internet and a special newsgroup, he's able to figure something happening with the country's imminent danger.

He's been following some encoded messages on his favorite newsgroup, alt.616. The newsgroup itself is symbolized from a Hebrew translation of the word Neron, as mentioned in the Bible. It supposedly represents the Emperor Nero. Whenever anyone uploads a new message, they're supposed to find some cryptic code and allow member subscribers time to figure it out before translating. The newsgroup originally started as 666, but everyone'd already had guessed the accepted erroneous translation. That's what Esther explains to me when we were isolated from people on our motel stay. And later on I find out something else.

Steve reviews new remarks daily on the newsgroup, and has been studying one in particular for the past several days. It originated in Norway and has a MSN return address. I couldn't translate even if someone told me what they said.

On CNN he's hearing about a submarine that has started its journey off the coast of Norway and has proceeded southward, thought to be headed for the Persian Gulf. He puts his thoughts together, and decides the sub has someone on board who is transmitting coded information to someone in New York. That's how the first message begins: "How is the weather on Long Island?" it reads.

On TV, CNN is now reporting that the Pentagon thinks the sub may have veered, and is in the Southwest Atlantic.

Again, Steve concludes that something is up at his folk's place, since he knows the president's brother is coming for a visit. He wants to leave the cabin and take the jaunt to Chapin, but he's also drawn to decoding possible new messages. He decides to wait it out till he hears from friends in Chapin.

In the meantime, he's worried about Esther. She usually calls just before she heads home. She's learned that the hard way, once being stranded overnight in a huge storm that crippled the entire region, felling trees, one of which destroyed the back end of her car. When she was rescued the following noon, all she could say was something in Gullah jibberish that she don't remember when I ask her.

***

Nearing final destination, Commander Lasting has his crew practice drills using two chambers that they will escape from at given intervals prior to scuttling the sub after launching missiles. He decides the best way to escape detection by radar is to remain deep below surface until the time of actual launch. Non-essential crew will be released in small rafts after dark, to be rescued by small boats whose destination has been pre-arranged. Only he and three crewmen will finalize the operation. His radioman will transmit the last signal before joining him in one of the escape chambers.

While surfaced at dusk, taking in a rising full moon, his radio operator extends antennas and transmits a message via the Internet to comrades in Tehran.

Unbeknownst to Commander Lasting, a message has also been sent to New York. Immediately, the operator deletes any copies of his message. He uses a wiping program that encodes several random encryption data over each deletion. Hard to reassemble on a captured hard drive.

Lasting has conceived an ingenious plan for using the Internet for undetected communication. No one, not even a set of individuals, is able to monitor every message sent by the minute on the Internet. Hardly anyone, particularly in the nation's spy monitoring network, bothers to investigate subversive newsgroups. Lasting has purposely used this clever method of communication to remain undetected until now.

He knows he's being tracked by radar, but also knows that he will not be intercepted unless he poses a direct threat to any nation. As far as anyone can know, the sub carries no nuclear armaments, and must be thought to be on a shakedown cruise. Indeed, he has zigzagged sufficiently, several times, so that Washington has concluded he will return to his original destination on each next turn eastward.

He has just released six of his crew to the surface above. At periscope depth, a small boat approaches, and he watches each man being lifted to safety. In minutes, the boat disappears from view and Lasting orders a new depth as he lowers the scope.

He trudges to his quarters, the combination of terror and conscience beginning its toll. Perspiration gathers on his upper lip and forehead. He wipes at both and enters. He looks up and reviews his rationalization on the wall of his bunker. Two news clippings reveal details of his possible court-martial. His picture is posted between two attractive females—one, a civilian, who has accused him of improprieties.

He reads passages he has highlighted in yellow marker: "Mrs. Daigle said that when her husband, Captain Elmer Daigle, approached her

on the subject, she admitted to the affair with
Commander Lasting. She said that it had taken
place over a three month period while her husband was on duty at Norfolk."

Lasting recreates mental images of his
amorous conquest. Helen Daigle, parading in a
sheer negligee he had purchased at Fredericks.
She didn't protest at all. Her husband had been
indifferent to her for weeks. She had come to
Lasting, her husband's superior officer, to see if
he could intervene. She knew it was the incor-
rect approach from the start, but since they had
fraternized socially, she thought he wouldn't
mind. The inevitable occurred. Lasting, freshly
divorced, was in his sport-fucking finest hour.
A panel concluded sexual harassment, in lieu of
adultery. Semantics.

He did not bother to peruse the other
highlighted passage, a report of similar details,
this time with the civilian daughter of a fellow
commander. Best he could recall, there were
five more women who had not stepped forward.

CHAP 25. Willie and Bo

We was supposed to have only one drink with meals, but on leaving the restaurant, Jack and Alma said we had come all this way to be entertained, and entertained was what we was gonna be. So Alma starts out for a liquor store she spots across the parking lot, and one of the agents, Ross, is yelling for her to stop.

"I'm getting something to drink for me and my guests," she turns and yells back. "You want to make a scene?"

He looks at Stark, the other agent, who motions to allow her to go, so we all follow. Both agents act pissed, but they probably feel like they've wondered why we haven't broken ranks before now, even with all the explanation they've provided. Only with the phone call did we give trouble, but they had already figured out we might do that, and had blocks put on everyone's cells.

Inside the store, Alma and Jack load up on exotic beers, and me and Lula buy some California wine.

"Esther?" Alma says.

"Sloe gin," comes back.

"Ugh," Alma makes a face and points to a pint on the shelf. The clerk adds it to one of three bags and we carry the stuff back to the van, with the Bible church sign still pasted to the side.

A woman in the parking lot has been following us with her eyes, and I turn around to see her shaking her head after the sliding door closes. Inside, Jack cracks a can of Foster's ale, and tells everyone he wants to eat at Outback if we're still all together tomorrow.

***

Back at the ranch, so to say, Willie and Bo, friends of Steve, turn their pickup along the last stretch of dirt road to Jack and Alma's place. Near the entrance they can see the yard full of cars. Willie has his black cap slung low on his forehead, its caption reads "Don't F--- With The Boss", in gold lettering. Just like that. Three letters left missing. Hard to figure. Beneath the rim, his hair sprawls over both ears meeting his T-shirt above a dingy collar. Through the open window, he flips an empty beer can backward into the pickup bed.

On the other side of the cab, Bo rests one leg atop the dash, the other beneath her bottom. She works at capping a fingernail with clear polish, while admonishing Willie to slow on curves. Twice she's had to clean and redo. She reaches one hand between her legs and tugs at tight-fitting yellow shorts, stretching them lower for more comfort. Her hair, freshly released from the confines of fifteen rollers, dangles like a yo-yo in harmony with undulating motions of truck springs on roadbed. It's been too long since the pickup suffered new shocks.

"Hmmm, must be having a party. We wasn't invited neither," Bo says, combing a lock of blonde hair.

When they pull into the driveway, a man steps from the bushes and holds a wallet up at arms length. He's dressed in a black suit with dark tie. It looks like an official badge to Willie, who stretches further from the cab window, while agent First steps on a high mound waiting for Willie to completely stop.

"Funeral?" Willie asks.

"No sir. Are you relatives of the Ripples'?" First says.

"Nope, just friends."

"Are Jack and Alma okay?" Bo slides on the seat next to Willie, distracting First's eyes to her bare thighs below short shorts.

"Yes ma'am. They are having visitors right now. May I ask that you return later perhaps?"

"When?" Willie spits tobacco to the ground, under the space of First's hand and arm, leaning on the cab top.

"Well sir, I don't know for sure. Do you have a number we can reach you at?"

"Shittin' aside, SIR," Willie says, "what the fuck is goin' on?"

"We're a special crew from a local television sir, doing a tape of a national exercise program, SIR," First ad-libs. He justifies his deception in his own mind.

"Yeah, right, and I suppose you're the chief guru," Willie says. "You got a gal named Esther here?"

"Ah, the Gulluh woman," First says. "No, she's decided to return home. I believe she lives in the northern part of the state. I believe I have her number in . . ."

"I already know it, or wouldn'ta asked," Willie says.

"Do you have an ID, or something?" Bo asks.

"Yes, ma'am, I'll show you again," First reaches into his coat pocket.

Bo can't make out the letters without glasses, and squints at the picture ID, a complete blur at four feet.

Willie says, "So, you ain't gonna let us in, I suppose. Well tell Alma and Jack we'll be back. And tell them that Steve is worried about Esther, okay?"

"Yes sir, I'll be glad to relay the message. And your names are?"

"Willie and Bo."

"Yes sir, and ma'am, thank you. Now if you'll turn through the driveway back to the road, I'd appreciate it."

Willie tracks the pickup through a grassy tire path, skidding his tires through the wet grass and reenters the semi-paved roadway. By the time he comes to the first stop sign, he's doing eighty. He runs through at about forty-five and is back to eighty again.

"Cut it hon," Bo warns, "We wanna be able to make it to the phone."

CHAP 26.The do-little brothers and the love of my life

It's funny how when you're in a uncomfortable situation like we are in this motel right now, how your mind goes back to something comfortable. I look around the room at my wife and friends staring, but not really watching TV. I bet the same is happening to them. For me, it's my past and sometimes present work I really enjoy, I'm thinking about.

Right now I'm thinking about the time I met these two brothers at a Basque feed in Elko. They said they lived up near Hole-in-the-Mountain. Had a spread that they bought back in the fifties, which, if I remember right now, was just about the time I met them. Late fifties.

After a couple more bottles of dago red, we got to talkin' pianos. They said they had one they'd like me to come up and tune. Had parties once in a while and one of the brothers liked to play *Rose of San Antone*, while one vocalized, adding a yodel. I was fresh out of apprenticing for a few years and had just opened my business in Reno.

Being used to the routine around Reno, I didn't even think to ask about the piano's condition before I decided to take the job. I was to regret that part of a memorable experience. It was a long way to go, but they said they could pay whatever I asked. I remember I could use the dough at the time to get the store open.

So I wrote the directions on the back of a napkin and said I'd be up the following Tuesday. My mother and me'd come over that way on Memorial Day to visit my father's grave. She said she could wait with some friends while I finished.

On Tuesday, I dropped my mother off and took some dirt roads off the highway near Deeth. Twenty-four dusty miles and umpteen fence gates with assorted hitching contraptions, I carefully guided my Rambler along the edge of a creek bed, dodging poplar tops downed from beaver work, while chasing trout upstream.

On a foothill plain here's what come into view: two Quonset huts, a log cabin, three work sheds, assorted vehicles, a John Deere, a D-6 Caterpillar, and other paraphernalia. I can't remember all of it, stretched for a quarter mile. I looked for the latest model car that might be running. Two were in front of the cabin, so I pulled alongside and parked. Two Collies greet me, one reaching to the edge of my window that's now half-open.

In seconds, the older brother, Ronnie, shows his face and dirty cotton flannel he's wearing through the doorway.

"You found it!" he seems surprised. "No worry, if you didn't show up by noon, we was a gonna start looking. Not a good place to be stranded."

"Dogs?"

"They'll lick ya ta death, all the way to Deeth," he chuckles.

When I get out, the slam of the car door sends a minor sandstorm skyward. While it descends, I extract my tool case from the back seat, this time closing the second door more gentle-like. No matter, this time small clods falling from the edge of rubber seals spread at my feet, garnishing another coat on already ruined Nunn-Bush shoes.

"Wanna beer?" Ronnie offers. It's nine-thirty a.m.

"Not before noon," I say. "Got some iced tea?"

"Nope, but we can make some."

"Fine."

"Where's the piano?" I say.

"In the add-on," he points from inside.

Hidden from the front entrance is a addi-

tion that looks completely different from the
rustic interior portion of the main cabin. We
walk through and go over to it. Ronnie must've
picked up on my look of surprise as my eyes
begin to compare what I was in, to what I can
see now.

"Bret's girlfriend," he says. "She's not
with him anymore. When he invited her to
come live with us, that was the condition."

"Gotcha," I say.

There's only one thing out of place in the
new addition. The piano. This can't be the one, I
think. A flush comes over my insides; Ronnie
tickles a couple keys and asks how it sounds. "I
don't play," bridges his effort with a stiff finger
roll along the trebles. "Bret's thing."

"This is it then?" I want to make sure.

"Un-huh. Whatta ya think, can you do it
Pilgrim?" he goes into a John Wayne imitation.

He waits for me to answer, and with
nothing seeming to dislodge communication
from my mouth, he adds, "I know, it's a bit
rusty and don't look too good, but we been
meaning to tune it for years. Bret says it ain't
that bad, even with a coupla broken strings."

"I'll do my best," I manage.

"That's what I like ta hear," he slaps at
my shoulder. "I'm gonna have a beer and then
it's to the woodshed for me. When you take a
break come on out. I think you'll wanna see
something. Bret's out with the cattle right now.
He'll be back 'fore noon. Stay for dinner."

Does he mean noon, or five? I'm thinking—*today or tomorrow?*

Getting to the "innerds", as he calls 'em, is easy. The lid, lower frame and fallboard have been carted away by either jackrabbits or beaver. When I remove the music shelf, I can hardly recognize tuning pins or upper string lengths for the dust. My eyes immediately shift to the room in search of a vacuum. I can't see none, so I return to my car trunk, dreading to retrieve and use my own. Shoulda thought about that a little longer. My fears ain't disappointing. Filling every crevice and weld in the trunk area, a thick layer of road dust blankets the entire inside. I mumble in vain, and slam the trunk lid without thinking again. Shouldn't have done that. Two weeks later, after cleaning almost daily, I'm still extracting Hole-in-the-Mountain dust from my car.

Back to the piano: I can barely make out the manufacturer, but think I can figure; it's an old Raymond. I don't think I've ever tuned another one like it since. Took it with them from somewhere in California where they used to live, I find out later. They come from the valley region south of Sacramento. Merced, I think one of 'em said. Hauled the piano from there years ago. Both played in a pick-up band when they was younger.

For a bit of time, in between my examinations, I survey pictures of the group hung on the wall in random locations. One thing I know right away. There's no use trying to tune a piano that's in need of major repairs and regulating. This was gonna be a lot longer than a day's work. I have to talk with Bret and Ronnie before starting.

A perfunctory vacuum job reveals felts that need new hide glue, seven strings broken in the trebles, one in the bass, four in midrange, several bent tuning pins, almost half the ivories missing (which could have been ignored), four broken hammer shanks, numerous rotted bridle tapes, uneven keys; all noted at first inspection and I haven't yet struck one key. What a surprise I get when I do.

I select one, tap it, and it yields a tin-like rattle. Upon examining the hammer felt, I extract a thumbtack. Inspection of several others reveals similar intended additions. I'd heard of the phenomenon, but had not seen it until now. To make pianos sound honky-tonk, tacks were added to felts to give a tinny sound. What else was I gonna find?

One final inspection, the most important far's I'm concerned, that of rust, would determine if I wanted to tackle the job at all. Fortunately in a dry climate like Nevada, rust is not a major problem. I've looked at jobs in Florida since moving there that I might a took, and walked out the door without saying good-bye. I looked around for something to sit on, and sank in for further inspection.

About an hour later, rising from a wicker stool piano bench, I go outside, and accompanied by two collies with tails wagging high, walk over to a Quonset to find Ronnie. Near the entrance, the sound of a chain saw echoes from metal corrugations. When I wade into the wide portal, look inside, my eyes feast on the unbelievable.

Easter Island in the East Humboldt Range. Figurines everywhere, carved from pine, cottonwood and poplar. Figurines hell; life-sized statues, some bigger. Solids and some laminated forms. Tools a restin' everywhere along several workbenches.

In the middle of gravel floor on a small stage, Ronnie stands with his arms folded around a chainsaw running at variable speeds, busily carving along a length of laminated cottonwood. Rippled saw marks grace his latest project. Think that's awesome? That's the new word I hear abouts these days. Wait'll I tell you the important part.

His work includes a model. A young woman dressed in native costume, that would be Native American I'm talkin' about, kneels low on a stand beside a steel tub filled with water, dipping her finger into the edge. On her head, a single feather. When Ronnie catches me in his view, he cuts the saw motor.

"*Springmaid*, I'm gonna call it," he says. "Saw it in a old magazine ad. *Saturday Evening Post*, if I recall. Done already?" he chuckles. Trying to stem my further questioning I figure.

"No—what in the world is this all about?" I can't help asking, looking around the hut at myriads of carved pieces, each with similar saw marks.

"My hobby. This is Lula," he introduces the young lady, "my cousin from Florida. Don't let her getup fool ya though. Not a Injun at all."

The lady smiles but don't say a word. I simply say hello, my tongue starting to form knots. I know right then I'm gonna have to become better acquainted with her though. By the end of the week, I would.

"This is gonna be a bigger job than I anticipated," I tell Ronnie. "'Bout three or four days worth. I'll need to use some of your tools maybe, also."

"Sure, can you stay?"

"And it'll cost ya," I add.

"Sure, no problem. You can bunk in the bedroom of the new addition. It's a guest room now since Bret won't use it anymore."

I'm wondering where the young lady is staying; an answer to that question I discover at the end of the first day when she scoots to a trailer perched up on the side of the nearest grade.

I watch as she makes the journey along a road that's been excavated to about halfway up the rise. Three of us guys sit on a shaded porch on the morning side of the cabin chugging beer; we watch her move like a spring doe. She looks back and waves occasionally. Ronnie waves back at her when she's got to the trailer door.

"Can't hardly climb that anymore," he says. "Don't know how I managed to get it there with the Cat."

"Almost didn't," reminds brother Bret.

He goes on to tell of how Ronnie had slipped from the edge of his own tracks, necessitating a cat-claw action down the steep slope to the bottom. He descended pretty fast at a haphazard pace. Bret had run from the Quonset when he saw Ronnie maneuvering, all the while fretting having to pick up his brother's remains in the creek bed.

"What does your cousin do?" I can't help myself.

"Still in college. Just come for a visit," Bret says.

"Un-huh," was all I can manage. Didn't want to seem too forward, but I sure was interested. The boys catch on right away, though.

"She's a looker, ain't she though?" Ronnie adds, and we all laugh. Yep, I'm thinking, she sure is that.

"So how's it going?" Bret asks.

"I tell him about replacing some strings first, splicing the broken bass till I come back with a new one in the future. I tell him I plucked the new ones to near tune so's to let them stretch till I got done with the rest of the work. I warn them that even after I'm finished, the new ones won't be done stretching, and that it'll be bothersome listening till I can come back and bring them up to pitch.

"Hell, no one around here'll know the difference," Bret quips.

"Speak for yo'self," Ronnie chimes.

They both act interested while I tell them how I've matched and glued hammer shanks,

supported by thread till the glue dries; how I've
carved and fitted three bass hammer felts to replace those chewed off by resident mice; how
I'll have to go over the complete action now
resting on a workbench in the Quonset.

I figure it's a good excuse to look over
the *Spring Maiden* a little closer in between my
tinkering. I add, I'm pleased that the sound-
board is intact; I think I've got just enough used
ivories to replace the ones missing on key tops.
They take turns guzzling new opened bottles,
alternately looking up as I describe my day's efforts. I'm hoping to keep them awake till I
finish my explanation. Really just trying to jus-
tify the bill I'm gonna have to charge.

"You still here on Friday?" Bret asks.

"I hadn't planned it," I say.

"Too bad. Why doncha stay one more
day, even if'n you're done."

"Yeah, one more," Ronnie adds. "Big
party Friday. Right here. Lula's gotta go back
on Saturday. Little going 'way celebration."

They don't have to encourage me too
much, but I act that way anyways. I'm a wanting to talk to this Lula gal more. Thought she
might be joining us after work some nights but
she don't. Says she a studying for some exams
up the trailer. We all respect her privacy after
hours while were sipping beer and telling lies.

Now's my chance, I figure, so I say okay.
They're paying for the entire job with two re-
turn tunings and regulatings, so why not.
Mom's having a good visit with friends any-

way. I've called her and she says stay, too, long's I want. No hurry about getting back. She's staying on a ranch over near Lamoille, and her friends is hoping she can stay the weekend she informs me.

Before Friday, I've had a chance to talk with Lula a coupla times, and on Thursday, we all go over to Stateline for eats. While pulling a few handles, one thing I seldom do, we get better acquainted. On the way home, we're sitting in the rear of Bret's Caddie, and I ask if she's seeing anyone. She says she's just broken up with someone. Says she needs a change of pace and that's why she come out from Kentucky. Gonna finish college in Reno. Lucky for me too, since that's where my new business is.

By the end of Friday night, we've become better acquainted, and at the shindig, we've danced to *Rose of San Antone* about five times. Fortunately, one of the guests plays a lot better than Bret, and Lula and I get a chance to dance a little closer.

Well you know the rest of the story, as the man says, and now I'm looking over at Lula who returns a bored sigh back at me. When is this over we're all thinking?

CHAP 27. Diving practice interruption

Maartha's making a dive into the deep of Lake Murray. She's following a hand-held searchlight with two Navy SEALs in tow. For the SEALs, justification is a tag-a-long.

Everyone's looking for any lost B-25 submerged during a World War Two training exercise while it's making a run on Bomb Island. There's supposed to be about twenty more strewn at random under the lake. Sonar has told them that this one is the shallowest.

Before she can get half-way to it, one of the navy men picks up a transmission on his headset, and swims to catch up alongside, motioning them, one by one, to turn back. He repeats for his compadre.

"Call from the house," he tells the First Lady when they arrive at the surface.

"What's Mr. President up to now?" Maartha inflects aloud, swimming to a boat hovering a few feet away. She's almost reached her underwater target and is anxious to continue. But she's also anxious about Ray and his dealing with the current situation. She's mad about being interrupted but is trying to contain herself best she can.

"They've located an important transition item ma'am," the SEAL leader says. Her mind starts guessing what he means, but she waits for an explanation, as the pontoon boat throttles to full. While the boat speeds, she studies underwater topology on a sonar instrument.

When they get back to the Ripples' home, a SEAL and two agents assist her from the boat. She releases herself from a grip on her elbow and skips along the lawn, dodging Canadian geese turds, until she gets to the back porch screened room. Just inside she purposely slams the door behind her. She wants it known that this is about her too.

In the distance, another boat is speeding toward the private dock with both daughters aboard. They've been dining in a cove that features a Tiki hut similar to one they've seen in the Florida Keys. A tin pan breakfast. They're bothered by the interruption too. Already a bunch of local guys have been asking for dates and telling where parties are gonna happen on the weekend.

"This had better be important, Ray," she does a faux glower at the president when she gets inside.

He's been interrupted too from his guitar practice in one of the bedrooms. He already anticipated he'd better get out to greet her when she comes in though, or she'll manage to upset the household.

The president pats the air ahead of him in a gesture to calm her. "Easy, easy, Maartha," he says. "You know we're all just trying to do our job here."

"So am I, Ray," she rips. "Just because you've managed to disrupt all our lives right now, does that mean we can't go on with our own duties and responsibilities?"

Everyone else leaves the living room area. When the daughters come up the pathway, they hear the argument and direct themselves toward a side entrance. They go into one of the back bedrooms and turn on the TV.

"This had better be good, Ray," Maartha continues. "I was almost at the site of the wreckage. Cameras were rolling."

"They've spotted a sub near the Bahamas," the president informs her.

Maartha slows her attack.

"Are the girls safe?" she asks. Her attitude is suddenly diverted from her own self-absorption.

"Yes, yes, I think we all are," Ray says. "I don't think anything would be directed toward us. It's reasonable to assume that the enemy doesn't know where we are."

"Enemy?" Maartha says.

"Yes, enemy, most likely terrorists. We've been following the sub for the last few days, and there's reason to believe that it's hostile. That's why we're here in the first place, also because of more direct threats to us of course. They still haven't found the New York group. I know it's not fair, hon. But look what they did to my concert too. I was just getting the new piece down when CNN broadcast the news from the Pentagon."

"How come we're waiting for the news to be on television before we get it?" Maartha asks.

"We're in hiding, remember?" Ray says. "That means no transmission or receiving of messages that could be intercepted and give our whereabouts. Those people are no dummies or we wouldn't be here in the first place."

"Hmmm," she says. "So how long do we stay inside?"

"We'll know as the news develops," Ray says. "As soon as we find out the intention of the sub, we'll know whether or not we've been compromised and got to take it out. Some Orion P-3C's are being sent on it right now. This could be over by the end of the day. Only thing left is the New York contact problem."

"Are you gonna tell me about that?"

"Not right now, Maartha. Just get your gear cleaned and ready, and if time permits, you can go back for another dive. Even if we're cleared, you can still stay for a couple of days to finish up. I know how important it is for you."

"Important for you, you mean," Maartha retorts. "This'll make for good propaganda on the hill, won't it Ray?" She sounds off a faux quotation, " 'First Lady Continues with Exercise Video in Spite of Threat', they'll all be saying."

"Now Maartha, when have I exploited you or the kids for political reasons?"

She backs off. "Okay, I'm sorry. It's just that this has all so disrupted my routine. I guess I should be used to it by now, but I still like to keep going on something once I've got it started. I won't be sorry at the end of your term, Ray, I gotta admit."

"I know, I know. While we're waiting, I'm going back to the bedroom. I can still get some time in before lunch. You wanna come back and listen to a couple pieces? I can still call it off, I guess."

"Not on your life," Maartha insists. "We aren't letting anything like those Arab shitheads affect our lifestyle. Besides, you know how everyone's been invited, and right now your friends are the most important. Don't you put it off for a second. Promise me Ray."

The President has no intention of postponing the concert, but it's a good chance to defer her abrasiveness by distracting her.

While Maartha strips away her wetsuit in a bathroom, the Navy SEALs are flushing her equipment with water from a garden hose and refilling canisters of air from a portable compressor. When finished, they wait in the pontoon boat for further instructions.

Although sound is somewhat muffled, everyone else, sitting glued to the television in the living room, can hear Ray practicing in the back bedroom. The sound of "Lagrima" drifts down the long hallway, blending into the right ear of agent Kennedy who's trying to listen simultaneously to the news broadcast.

Ray quickly shifts to a few bars of each piece in his repertoire. He wants to recall each selection without referral to the published program. Most of the pieces are standard fare, heard by guitar enthusiasts the world over. Only one new selection, and he's considering deletion or saving for an encore. He's got apprehension about doing the "Leyenda" number. Doesn't like the way his fingers are trying to coordinate the passages.

CHAP 28. Good news and bad

At The Roses motel, seven people have watched the same news on TV.

"I suppose that's why we're here," Lula Galway comments.

Neither agent responds.

Communication is taking place on a side road not too far from the Ripples' home.

***

"Something's up," Willie speaks into the receiver. "When we got there, they wouldn't let us come in."

"Are you shitting me man? I thought they had forgiven you by now," Steve says.

"No man, not your folks—the FBI."

"FBI? What the hell is the FBI doing at

my folks's place?"

"That's just it. Says they were making a movie. Very hush-hush. Your folks agreed so they said."

"Did they show you ID?"

"'Course, for Christ's sake. You think I'd let someone get by with that?"

"Okay man. Thanks. Another favor. I'm coming down right away if I can get the pickup started. If not it'll be a bit longer. In the mean-time, can you go to the local police and get them checked out. I just want my folks to call me, okay? You didn't see Esther?"

"Nope. They did say she was around though."

"This doesn't make any sense at all. She never told me about a movie or anything. I'm coming down. I'll stop at the police station first. I'm not sure, but somehow I gotta feeling that this is tied up with what's going on right now."

"What's that?" Willie says.

"Christ man, ain't you been watching TV? It's all over the Internet. Some Iranians or Russians or both are getting ready to attack us I think. There's a submarine anchored somewhere near Cuba. They think it has a nuclear arsenal and we're about ready to get it. Better take Bo and hide in the hills somewhere. Hell, come on up here. We can go over to Table Mountain and find some caves."

"No shittin'?"

"No shit man. Turn on a television when you get home. I gotta go try start the pickup.

See you in a couple."

"Okay. If we ain't here, we'll be camped down the road from your folks. Maybe we'll take a boat out and see what we can see."

"Okay, see you there in a while. Hi to Bo."

"Bye man." Willie hung the phone and returned to his pickup. Together he and Bo sped toward the police station in Chapin.

***

By now, agents at the motel have set up a laptop and are corresponding with agents at the Ripples' home using instant mail.

"How's the weather?" agent Ross clicks the 'SEND' button.

"A little overcast," Kennedy returns.

"Here somewhat too," Ross replies. *"Another long day?"*

"Hope not. Want to finish fishing before the storm comes in," Kennedy writes.

"Got your limit then?" from Ross.

"Will know after I let a little more line out," Kennedy continues.

And so on, till enough information becomes transmitted and received between the two agents. At the end of the conversation, Ross lowers the television sound and speaks to the group.

"There's some good news and some bad," he says. "Which first?"

"The bad," Alma says.

"I knew it would be you," says Ross. "There'll be a lot of cleanup to do when we're through with your place."

"An' de gud?" Esther asks.

"We may have this phase wrapped up by the end of the day. Sub chasing aircraft are on their way right now. If we keep watching, CNN may have a live broadcast."

"That mean we go home?" Jack asks.

"We think so sir. We've got a full day paid up though, if you want to stay around."

"Yeah, right," Lula adds.

"Well, let's not let it go to waste," I try. "How about a last rubber of *Oh Shit,*" I ask the group. Right away, about twenty used plastic cups assault my being. We're all beginning to wonder how much of our ruse has leaked to the outside by now.

Outside the room, whenever we peek through the edge of the curtains, we see maids are talking among themselves, looking over in our direction. Every time they knock for cleaning, we all gather and begin a prayer. A couple times they've made excuses to leave and come back. True to our mission, they find us with hands folded, looking skyward. They're having trouble with this. Seven people in a bunch a motel rooms in the middle of the week praying their heads off. In between gospels, we're all studying the TV.

How did a sub get through without detection? The pundits are asking on every channel. Greta and Roger are having special broadcasts. Geraldo is having another orgasm. Conversations and hypotheses begin to develop among us.

I'm thinking it's easy.

***

Following the cold war and plans for disarmament beginning in the early nineties, the U.S. had already established funds to help Russia disassemble and destroy nuclear weapons. A huge accident of nature occurred at a submarine base in Severodvinsk, when a mountain, tumbling courtesy of gravity, buried much of the in-place construction.

Why watch subs any more? SOSUS was already getting unreliable. Attention became directed skyward with deployment of satellites to better monitor hostile activity on any surface of the globe. Let the Russians make and refurbish subs for foreign purchase. It would mean we'd have to loan them less. Even Orion upgrades were being budgeted backwards. If a deviant sub did become suspect, it could be easily approached, intercepted and dispatched—so everyone thought.

Right now *global warming* is more important. In traditional mode, the country has become complacent, and now the president and family are in hiding because of it.

***

One of these days, someone or something has to get through our defenses. Right now is another try. We're about to get an update on television.

There it is. The maid is in the room and we're all in prayer, but someone, I think it was

Lula, ups the sound. The maid looks up with
the rest of us. She's distracted enough now not
be able to care about our scam.

On the screen, from the window of an
Orion aircraft, someone has a camera focused
on the ocean. From the pilot's vantage, a faint
outline of something that looks like a giant
whale comes into view. It's barely under the
surface. Right before our eyes, the television
screen gets jostled, and in the next view a big
explosion comes through the surface of the water. A giant plume vaults skyward. It's all
recorded and the maid asks what movie we're
watching.

"Whoa, that's not us," the pilot is overheard to say. "All missiles secured."

"All missiles secured?" Ross looks over
at his fellow agent.

Have we blown the buggar up or what?
is what I'm thinking.

CHAP 29. Crisis temporarily over

Confusion reigns on every channel. In the middle of a soap opera on another television that we had brought in from a rental, an interruption switches to a local station out of Columbia. It's the same news that we've been watching on the other set.

Conclusions are reported that are later to prove erroneous.

A newscaster is speaking:

"It appears that a navy attack airplane, an Orion P-3C out of Jacksonville, has destroyed a submarine that appeared to be a threat on Washington. Reliable sources say that this submarine was armed with nuclear threat able to be deployed with multiple warheads set to strike several cities along the Atlantic seaboard.

Among those is Washington, and nearby Camp David where the president has gone with his family for undisclosed mid-week meditations. Sources also confirm that the president and First Lady sought early release of their two daughters from college when a family crisis developed. It is said that a possible death in the family, the president's sister-in-law, a Mrs. Lula Galway from Florida was the reason for the retreat to Camp David."

Hey folks, Lula's right here beside me. Course, when Lula hears the news first hand, she immediately tells me to remember to tell the Social Security Office soon's we get back, not to send her checks any more. We all have a laugh on that one.

"Where do they get all this stuff?" she asks agent Ross.

Ross immediately gets her drift and becomes defensive. "No ma'am, it didn't come from us," he tells her.

The phone rings in Ross's pocket and he begins a series of *un-huhs* and *rogers* then folds the phone.

"Late tonight, about ten," he informs us all. "We can head back. Bet you're all relieved."

"Does this mean this is all over?" Alma asks.

"We think so. They're trying to wrap things up. Sorry for the delay and inconvenience."

I'm just glad my brother and his family are out of the quicksand. Now I suppose we can continue on to Washington, although I haven't got word if Ray is still gonna go through with the White House invite. No sense asking Ross. He's pretty closed mouth about everything except a need-to-know argument.

"What's for the last supper?" I say.

"Whatever and wherever you like," he answers.

"Okay, how about *Outback*? I'm ready for about a pound of juicy beef, a bloomin' onion and four mugs of Foster's. Make it more than juicy—I want to kill the cow myself."

Ross looks around. Nobody is objecting.

"Okay, lets load up."

It takes everyone about forty-five minutes after the go 'head to assemble at the van. Mostly potty breaks and hairspray. Before getting in, Lula asks about the church sign still pasted to an outside panel.

"Take it down," Stark says. Everyone "yeas".

All the way to Columbia, Stark is on his cellular, Ross is paying attention to driving in heavy traffic. We've definitely left at the wrong time. Work traffic is our competition for road space.

Me, I'm sitting in front this time. "We gonna be able to meet with the president before he leaves?" I ask Ross. I always use the unfamiliar reference whenever I talk to anyone about my brother.

"I'm not sure sir, but in your behalf I've anticipated the question and am awaiting a reply."

"Thanks. Let me know as soon as you can," I say, though I don't know why I said it. There's no hurry to know on my part. Either we can, or we can't.

***

Back at the ranch, about an hour later, Ray and family are getting into station wagons that will take them to the 'copters at the rec center ball fields. The same attendants who first greeted them have been called in to monitor traffic. They'll be offered extra pay that they'll probably refuse.

We find out later, the crisis ain't over yet. Although they'll be back at the White House before morning, operatives in New York and Baltimore haven't been fully identified or apprehended. There still might be a threat to the president's person. The president and family will be under heavy security for the next several days.

***

At just before midnight we get back to the Ripples' place, where we're greeted by security lights in the yard when we pull into the drive. Other than the blinding lights, all is quiet. In the house, lights are on and two maids are busily cleaning the place. When we walk in, there's plastic garbage bags half full everywhere you look.

Alma asks how long they're gonna be. About another hour, one says. If we can all wait on the back porch, it will be appreciated. They ask Alma where clean sheets are stored. They'll make up all the beds and start a wash.

We're all dog-tired by now, and full of steak and Foster's. But we manage to hang out and raid the extra refrigerator on the porch like we need it. Ross and a different agent, whose name I can never remember, Mc Harrington or something like that, begin their farewells, thanking us for our cooperation and telling Lula and me they'll look forward to seeing us in Washington by week's end. They get in a rental and we watch tail blinkers signal a right turn out of the driveway. They're headed for the airport in Columbia. Stark's already took off.

"Mucker anyone?" I joke. This time I get a round of used napkin trash thrown at me.

When the maids wrap it up, they leave and we all go inside. There's still an odor of cigarette smoke, though a country-fresh carpet deodorant has been sprinkled to mask it all. "Your nieces," Lula says under her breath standing next to me.

"Proof?" I say. She ignores me, walking ahead to our usual bedroom.

A car pulls into the yard. The slam of a pickup door resonates throughout the household. He doesn't bother knocking. I hardly recognize him through a full beard and mopped curly hair. "You okay?" Steve greets his mother. His dad shakes a hand and Esther runs to his arms.

"Where fo'de be'n?" Esther says, half Gullah and half Shakespeare.

We all talk briefly and me and Lula make excuses to retire. In a few minutes, we hear Alma and Jack come down the hall past our bedroom. Five minutes later, the roar of a bad muffler is heard in the yard and for thirty seconds, its echo is heard blasting through the surrounding woodland. Esther will explain to Steve on the way back to Sassafras. The hyperbole will undoubtedly come out in Gulluh-speak.

CHAP 30. Leftovers

When we wake up, it's Friday. We've got to be in Washington by Sunday. That is, if the invite and concert is still on. Ray has left a message that we're to come. He says it's still a go, far's he's concerned. Feels strange to be back to almost normal in Jack and Alma's house again. Like a nightmare just happened. Went by so fast, we really didn't visit like we wanted to.

We'll spend the day with Jack and Alma, then head out in the morning. A day's drive. I like driving a trip on Saturdays. Everyone's still doing the Friday-night-work-hangover and the roads are clear. What's left is local shoppers doing home projects; mothers taking kids to lessons; dads emptying yard trash and mowing lawns; aunts doing Wal-Mart for last minute birthday presents; kitchen help decorating birthday cakes for the afternoon party, and so on. Me and Lula will have the interstate all to ourselves, that is, until about one, when everyone will be driving to the beach. We'll get on the road early. Say our good-byes before bedtime tonight.

One thing the maids didn't get to do. The pontoon boat that we want to use for an early evening trip to a cove restaurant is still littered with diving gear. We don't even know who it belongs to. We figure that the girls must've rented it for some scuba diving to relieve their boredom while here. Wasn't till later we found out different. There's a similar label on each piece of equipment, however, and by afternoon Jack has located the outfit in Columbia. They'll come out and get it for a fee, or we can return it by Tuesday, when the rental expires. Jack says he'll bring it back. Funny the FBI guys didn't take care of it. I guess some things do get by them once in a while.

We're still glued to the television in the afternoon to see the latest developments. They still haven't caught more suspects they're after in New York, Baltimore, and now they're saying Philadelphia too. No one is still able to figure what these support people have to do with the destroyed sub. But they say the president is at Camp David and in a few minutes will be arriving back at the White House. We can all watch to see him and the rest of the family deplane on the lawn. Funny how reporters now have to cover up their own stories.

There's new news. Someone wants to dispel the rumor that the president's sister-in-law has passed away. It's been an erroneous report. I look over at Lula and she seems relieved. She starts passing around her body parts for everyone to feel. We start asking her how it feels to be back from the grave. Did she see the bright light that everyone who's been there and back seems to report? Lula goes on a fiction-frenzy and starts a story about her journey to the nether land. At the conclusion she says she might get a children's book out of her experience. We wonder what Ray is going to say to reporters greeting the family as they arrive.

The president isn't talking and they usher him into the back door quick-like. He's already arranged for Maartha to be interviewed and she's jumped at the chance.

She begins by telling the world that the experience has left her somewhat tired but that it gave her some time to spend with the girls and to work on several new routines that will be revealed to the young people of the nation. Especially those who want to remain young. She's glad that the threat to the White House has been thwarted and she's looking forward to the president's concert on Sunday. Right now she wants to review some tapes and get a shower so she excuses herself. And the daughters, who have simply garnished the interview by standing at her side, are escorted into the White House.

Leaving the bouquet of microphones, an agent hands her what appears to be a long curved bar of flat iron. She grips it in one hand and carries it like a ski while she walks to the house entrance. She turns and waves it at the crowd of reporters. Some are yelling for an explanation. We're all wondering, what in the world, and look at each other around the room when we see it.

"An exercise prop," Lula says.

"Naw," the harmony replies.

"I'll bet," she counters.

***

About a year ago when Maartha started this stuff, she was visiting a nearby armory and decided to do a video using an army rifle. It was one of the best she's ever done. She didn't realize at the time the impact it would have.

Several girls around the country did juvenile time in local lockups because they had carried a rifle to school for the purpose of instructing classmates *a la guru* Maartha. Some were pep squad members. Local police confiscated tapes, searched the girl's homes and investigated parents before the news got sufficient evidence that the youths were simply using Maartha's paradigm. Like that word Lula Anne? School violence in the nation's immediate past had imported new rules that officials followed religiously if not judiciously.

Upon hearing about the incidences, the First Lady made a national live appearance before the cameras, telling the young ladies that while exercise was very important, it would perhaps be better to emulate one of her other tapes. Especially one where she wears chaps and shimmies up a twelve-foot pole, and shows how the move can be used with alternative standing objects, like a backyard tree. She extended the idea, later on, when she went to New Hampshire on one of Ray's primaries. Think I already covered that.

I could see the young kids back home at the time. Young ladies just out of school in Battle Mountain, looking over a nearby Russian olive tree, contemplating whether to put on leather chaps or rough it.

The pole stuff started when Maartha and Ray took their first visit back home to Nevada after he became president. They were looking over colleges with the girls at the time. While visiting with friends in California, Maartha got interested in the work of a friend's husband. He was living in the Mother Lode region, and had an antenna business. Some of his work involved climbing two hundred feet up using lineman gear, topping a tree, putting up an antenna and rappelling down the side with a rope. Daring Maartha asked if she could make a trip with him. Ray was with the girls, visiting Stanford at the time, or he probably would've kyboshed the idea.

So she climbs up a smaller tree with the friend. He tops the tree, ties a hitch and wraps a sling around them both for descending. They both come ripping down the tree with the cameras on them, and at the bottom, the only thing he's holding with his arm around her when they land is her left breast. He's asking her if she's okay, all the while forgetting where his hand is while the cameras are still rolling. When he comes to, he's embarrassed, apologizes, and yells to get the cameras off. It's too late. Maartha's just laughing up a storm over it all, and wants to keep it in, but in deference to the friend, decides to scrap it. Ray tells me all this stuff later by long distance calling from a meeting at the university in Reno. That's how she gets the idea for the pole video, and later, one she uses like a inverse pendulum.

CHAP 31. Retrospeak

A navy man from Annapolis is being interviewed during prime time on a special concocted by CBS. Already, "60 Minutes" has finagled two extra time slots on TV. One on Wednesday and one on Friday. They're getting ready for a third. Every other news report on television has become an extended special. There's no more ordinary news for anyone to watch, except for the locals. Many of them also have gone to extended time. That's what television has become. There's such a lack of creativity that everyone is trading on instantaneous excitement in their daily lives to relieve the boredom. The virtual realty of live news reports. It's out there news anchors—go dig.

Even kids are watching CNN on school TV. Students are giving up lunchtime to remain indoors. Substitute teachers are being hired to monitor rooms, where sets have been installed so that news broadcasts can be viewed throughout the day, plus two extended hours beyond the school bus limit.

One kid has managed to remain in the restroom until all others have gone, and what does he do—pilfer the Home Ec classroom? Naw, he goes back into the room that he's been in all day, and turns on a news channel.

And at our lakeside television, two reporters are interviewing an ex-commander and the Naval Academy submarine instructor. It's enlightening stuff.

Newsman1: How would you compare the "boomer" we sent out, to the new Severodvinsk?

Commander: No comparison. The Russian sub is not on line yet.

Newsman2: Oh, so you're saying it wasn't a Severodvinsk that was encountered.

Commander: Not a chance, they couldn't have accelerated to that capacity by now. Chances are it's a Yankee or Typhoon class. Most probably a Typhoon, since that's what we were tracking from Barents a few weeks ago. At least that's what Busy One subframes have told us.

Newsman1: Busy One?

Academy: B-S-Y dash 1. A lead process computer that not only is able to direct activities to other computers, such as VLS's and MIRVs, but with employment of new COTS's systems, can act on GPS's, through USSTRATCOM. Even a nuke is now trained in TWPs to employ MADs.

Newsman1 glances at newsman2, an eye signal is exchanged, and Academy has been voted out of the inner circle.

This is what the kids and navy submarine personnel want to watch. The rest of the navy is still enjoying shore leave. Every submarine base, from Norfolk to Bangor, is taping the program so that videos can be added to the library aboard new *boomers* for extended-duty viewing later. Copies will be intermingled with other titles, for example: "Don Knotts Goes West".

About ten more minutes of concentrated discussion with the commander and Academy goes ballistic. He manages to rejoin the conversation and won't be headed off again. He's academic and begins with what he's conditioned for. He tells about BESS; how it trains XOs, EMs, ICs, and MMs; regroups DSRVs; utilizes QMs for long missions in unitizing EABs. A dirge of related acronyms in a thirty second effusion. A few patronizing words and a news anchor shifts back to the commander.

Newsman2: So, Commander, what we're saying is that we don't know, and really won't know what kind of sub, the way you put it—an SSN, SSBN or NSSN the sub was. The newsman has caught acronym fever from Academy.

Commander: That's right. And we probably will never know, that is, unless we're curious to find out by diving something into about four miles of seawater.

Newsman2: Does the commander of the sub have a name yet, sir?

Commander: Not that I've heard. But we're trying to get that track.

Newsman1: Isn't there another sub in that region on the bottom, the K-219?

Commander: That's right, and this one is not too far from it. At least that's the coordinates we have right now.

Newsman1: Tell me whatever happened to the nuclear capability of that K-219, Commander? Does it just remain on the bottom deteriorating through the ages? Is there any danger of ocean contamination in our immediate future?

Commander: You'd have to consult with authorities who are more proficient in disarmament than I am to answer that question.

Academy wants to interject, but Newsman2 cuts him off right away and the program switches to a commercial.

***

Lula and me have our bags packed, have taken evening showers and are ready to get out at daybreak. We've told Alma and Jack that we'll come by on the way home next week sometime. We'll call first.

***

The phone rings at about five in the

morning. We find out later that it was son Steve. He's called his parents to tell them they've arrived on the mountain safely. Good for you Steve, I'm thinking. Probably the best place to be at any time during the present century. I'm beginning to wish I'd of stayed in Nevada. Course, we've got a lot of munitions stored out there too that would make a feasible target in the event of another conflict.

Steve's call is a signal for us to get up. We particularly like driving in the early a.m. A lot of the truckers are getting an early morning snooze and we can usually crank out a hundred miles before they get busy. But once they're on the highway, it's alert time. More and more trucks crowding the highways every day. Television and newspaper ads are having enlistment programs.

Five hundred dollars down, and in six weeks you can become an experienced trucker. You too can learn the ins and outs of parallel driving in both left lanes, thereby creating a jam of cars behind while you and your buddy talk on CB.

***

At six forty-five we've done our hundred miles and stop to eat in Charlotte. Only about four hundred more to go. We should be there by late afternoon, that is, unless the Beltway uses up a couple extra hours. We haven't driven in the region for a few years, but Ray has given us advanced warning. Course we haven't figured on traffic much.

In the restaurant, every eye seems glued on television. This time, it's a local channel that's deferred to national news. Anchors are reporting that through the efforts of someone at sea, someone using a wireless transmitter with e-mail capabilities, foreign agents in New York have been located and a terrorist ring has been captured. Scratch one more threat.

CHAP 32. Meditations

We make the White House by five-thirty. The Beltway has been horrendous, like Ray told us. Lula was all for pulling into the nearest motel about two hours ago, but I managed to talk her out of it. I don't usually put my foot down, because she's most often right about stuff. But this time, I told her I had come all this way to spend a night in the White House, and nothing was going to deter me. What a mistake that kind of thinking was to be.

We get to the front gate, tell the guys on duty who we are and wait for ten minutes while one is making several phone calls. He comes back to the car window and tells us that arrangements have been made to stay at the Watergate, and starts to give us directions and a city map. I stop him mid-sentence.

"Look, can I speak with my brother directly?" I say.

"I'm sorry, Mr. Galway, but the president isn't available right now, sir. His secretary directed us to inform you about your quarters, sir," he answers.

"Well, can you tell me he's okay?" I ask.

"Oh, yes sir, the president is fine. He's meeting with officials is what we've been informed, sir. Members of his cabinet I believe, sir. That makes him unavailable at this time. Should the situation change, sir, we've got your information and location and will notify you immediately at the president's request. Now, sir, if you could simply make the loop and follow the map directions, you will wend your way to your quarters. There's an excellent cafeteria across the street from your location that I can recommend. Of course, room service at the Watergate is excellent as well."

Where in the hell did this guy get his training, I'm thinking, at the *Department of Diplomacy*? Is there some new cabinet post that we're all paying for that we don't know about?

I hand the map routing to Lula who's a better navigator reading a map than I am. There's no sun out right now. She's been to Washington before and up and down the East Coast several times. Where I grew up, geography, specially map reading, wasn't one of the subjects stressed. One thing though we did learn—east from west. If I tell Lula we're heading east, she always asks how I can be sure. The sun, I say. Suppose it's cloudy, she'll answer. There's still enough light coming in to be able to tell, I answer. Suppose it's dark out? Then you remember what direction you started with and how many turns you made in the interim. Where did you learn *that* word? she'll say. And we get into a nonsensical argument. We're both good at that.

I almost get crunched a couple times by other cars while we're driving to the hotel. Not only am I not used to driving in this awful traffic, but my mind is elsewhere. How is Ray gonna find time to practice at the last minute for his concert, I'm thinking.

I remember those kids and teachers in college when I had the piano contract. They'd want me out of the place two days before they're ready to perform. Course they'd want me back about an hour before the performance, for a fine-tune. But they'd be all nervous and on edge, going over movements in their heads and all. It's gotta be a lot of stress.

I can't imagine how Ray's handling it right now with all he's got to get ready for. Maybe that's why he's been panned with what some critics say is mediocrity in his playing. He don't care about them though. He says he's got his fans among the people in the nation who want to hear him anyway. I'm thinking, that Liberace had his same kind of critics, but was pretty popular with the folks during his time.

At the same time, I think I understand

what the critics mean. It's hard for someone, to study, perfect one's trade and have someone else, who doesn't know or give a damn about any of it, to understand. What does the every-day dude coming home from a day at the office know about the work of the plumber, who's made a house call to pack a washer on a cus-tomer's cold water tap, or care about how it came out? He'll know he's been there all right, soon's he gets the bill. But how did the plumber know how much packing in the form of a spe-cial long piece of oakum would be just right? Years of study, thinking and experience went into it. That's what the homeowner is paying for.

I remember reading about some guy back when coal furnaces used a lot of conductive pipe to get the heat to flow somewhere. The "Sup" gets a call from a tenant that she's not getting any heat to her apartment. Of course, it's the middle of the night. When he arrives and listens to her complaint for five minutes, he says he can fix the problem but it'll cost her twenty-five bucks. She agrees and follows him to the basement. When they arrive, he takes the palm of his hand and taps a conduit near a flap valve. "That's it," he says. "You've got heat."

"You mean you're gonna charge me twenty-five dollars for that?" she says. "Item-ize, please."

"One dollar and twenty-seven cents for calling me out in the middle of the night; the rest for knowing where to tap," he says.

We're stuck in traffic and haven't ate since early lunch. Worse time we could've been caught in the city.

Ray don't know didley about his guitar; its construction, that is. Oh sure, he's told me how some guy named Schneider made it, how he's named it and all, but looking at the mechanics of the instrument, he just knows a lot went into it to make it what it is.

I remember when he first told me about it. He was the Gov then, and had just saw an ad for the instrument in some classical guitar magazine. We always liked to compete in knowing stuff about what each other was doing, so I took the time to look up a few names at the library and to visit with some friends who repaired instruments. We had traded a lot of techniques that I used in some of my piano repairs. Especially stuff about cracked soundboards and the like. Guitars and pianos have a lot in common that way.

Anyway, one of my friends told me about this professor from Florida State University, a molecular physicist of some sort, if I got it right, who had been working part-time on making the best sounding guitar. He even wrote a book about it. I asked my friend if I could get a copy. He said no, it hadn't been published, but he had a copy of the draft that the guy, I think his name was something like a cereal I like to eat, had sent him. At the time, my friend was making guitars and thought the correspondence might lead to something. So he loaned me his copy and I read it.

Next thing I know, the guy has collabo-
rated with this Schneider fellow and they're
making guitars for sale. Some of them endorsed
by Segovia. So next chance I get, I tell Ray
about all this stuff, how special formulas and
bracing have been used; how placement of the
bracing has been designed to enhance base and
treble tones; how changes in thickness of the
fret board on the base side has been trimmed to
account for the extra amplitude in string vibra-
tion, and a lot of technical stuff that I can relate
to the piano.

When I'm telling Ray all this, he's nod-
ding like he understands, but I know he really
doesn't, see. He thanks me, and decides he's
gotta have one of those guitars, but he really
doesn't understand the workings. I understand
the workings, but can't play a lick. It's like the
piano. I can't play a lick of that either, but I
know how to tune one, regulate it and keep it in
fine repair. Maybe if I *could* play, I'd understand it a lot better.

Likewise, if Ray tells me about something that's nationally, or internationally
important, I have trouble understanding all of
the intricacies. He's made a lifetime of perfect-
ing his trade, which is diplomacy, I guess.
Everybody has his own fine-tuning routine in
that business. They all understand one another,
but nobody on the outside understands them.
Lots of the pundits on television will act like
they do; but then, they're not really there mak-

ing the decisions every day, now, are they?

CHAP 33. A switcheroo

We got here and have nice accommodations. We took the guard's suggestion and walked over to this basement cafeteria not too far away and had a good supper, though I'll probably have trouble sleeping from that piece of apple pie smothered with whipped cream.

Lula's reading all the brochures she found in the lobby and asking me if I want to visit some of the landmarks over the next few days. I tell her I'm pooped from all this hassle and just soon get back home. I use "missing the cat" for my diversion to act like a barn horse.

There's nothing to do in this hotel but wait. Like maybe somebody'll show up and make life interesting or something.

It's about eight when someone from

Ray's office calls us. He says we're to be at the White House at about noon tomorrow for an informal luncheon followed by the performance. He didn't say whether or not chow was with Ray. What're we gonna do till then? I watched enough TV in The Roses in South Carolina to last me a lifetime. Looks like I'm in for more anyway.

So Lula and I rent some videos and spend the rest of the evening watching. At least *I'm* watching. She's found a couple books to read at a small bookstore we passed by on the way back from the restaurant. It was a video rental store at the same time.

The clerk said we could leave them at the hotel desk when we were done. Just my luck I'll get a bill for them next month after some night clerk swipes 'em.

Neither one of us sleep all night. We've had a late snack in bed after calling for room service. So I end up watching one of the rentals twice while Lula puts a pillow over her head to block the television glare.

Next day at about eleven thirty, we get a call from the front desk. Someone's here to pick us up. Our rooms have been rented for an indefinite period we're told.

We've been ready since five a.m. Lula looks at herself in the full-length mirror once more, takes a turn at adjusting my tie and we go the elevator.

When the door opens, and we walk out to the street, a greeter nods to a limo driver who's accompanied by some other guy in a neat suit with a wire headed from his collar to his ear. Another agent, no doubt, but not the same guy I remembered from a couple days ago. Or was it yesterday? I keep losing track this week.

When we arrive at the same gate like the night before, the guard passes us right through and we end up in some side door to the White House. Inside, the agent asks if we'd like some refreshments before lunch, so I order a beer. Lula high-signs me. I cancel the order. She asks for two iced teas, sweetened.

We're escorted to another room where a bunch of people is gathered and finally I recognize someone. My two nieces come over to greet Lula and me.

"Hi uncle Ed," Rayette, the older one says to me. "Hi Aunt Lula."

Marthine, the younger one, is quiet and a little standoffish. She just nods at both of us and turns to catch the eye of an intern standing against a doorframe.

"Where's your folks?" Lula asks, affecting a drawl that I thought she got rid of long ago.

"They're still in a meeting," Rayette says. "Daddy hasn't slept most of the night and he's been trying to practice."

"What time's he on?" I ask.

"Oh, there's been a change," she says.

"See, we're not actually going to see him playing. They're going to have some other guitar player substitute and we're going to watch

him. Later, Daddy's going to play and make a
tape that will be combined with the one they
make of us watching, and that's the one that'll
be shown on T.V."

"You mean we've come all this way to
visit and watch your daddy play for us, and
we're not going to see him in person?" Lula
says, her accent gone.

"I don't understand exactly what you
said, Rayette," I tell her, which I don't. I'm still
trying to get the picture, when Marthine adds to
it.

"You see, Uncle Ed," she starts, "our dad
is in no shape to perform live right now. There's
still some confusion about some possible assassins that might be loose after the submarine
fiasco. So what they're going to do, is make a
tape of his guests watching a live performance,
then later, dad is going to do a tape of his program. The two will then be meshed by experts
and combined to produce the live performance."

"They can do that?" I'm still stupid.

"Oh sure, Uncle Ed," she says, " They do
it all the time."

"Then how can they call it live?" I say.

"Cause it is, Uncle Ed. We're watching
live, and Daddy is performing live. It doesn't
mean we are simultaneously live."

Both girls have a laugh over Marthine's
last comment. Rayette says that she's never seen
a comment or heard of one where the announcer says, "Now—*simultaneously* live, from

the ballroom of, . . ." And they giggle once more.

"So where is this taking place?" Lula is getting impatient, her new shoes already starting to cramp her toes.

"Right in the next room," Rayette says. "You wanna go in now?"

I get Lula's message that she wants to sit. The shoes. After we're introduced to a bunch of people that I've only seen occasionally on television, we go in. I know Lula is begging a chair so she can take off those damn shoes. Evidently, lunch has been postponed till after the concert, so we're told. The guitarist has this time slot only open.

Inside we're seated next to someone that both girls recognize, and they come over for autographs. I later learn that they're some sort of guitar experts, or critics or the like.

An emcee climbs a small platform and tells us what's gonna happen. A guitarist, a local fella from Georgetown music department, will be performing. When the applause sign goes on, we're to follow the cue. Occasionally the camera will pan the audience, doing close-ups, in which case we're to look like we're enthralled with what's going on. Yeah, Lula'll like that one too.

The guy explaining is all hand motions, and I'm picturing he's got a hair salon on the side. No need to be concerned that the president isn't the actual performer. Later, he'll do his thing, and tape editors'll take care of the rest.

It's all hocus-pocus to me, but I'll play along. Free dog and pony show. We can wait another hour or two to see Ray.

CHAP 34. The substitute

I look at the program and recognize the first piece. It's one that Ray has done many times, and one that our mother loved. It was written by Ray's favorite composer, Tarrega, and is impressive so Ray says, because of the coordination and control it appears to impart. He's told me on several occasions when I heard him play it. I'd have to look it up to say it right, even then with my Spanish accent wouldn't sound right. It means, like memories of some theater or art museum, or something like that.

So this guitar player shows up in tails, just like Ray would, and waits till everyone's quiet. Guitar players are real fussy about quiet, worse than piano players, I'd say. Well, the instrument is a lot softer. Some get real mad about *quiet*.

I remember attending a concert with Ray at the University of California at Davis when Segovia came to town. We drove all night to get there, Ray holding ticket reservations all the way down from Elko. When the performance started, about five measures into the piece, someone in the audience sneezed. Ol' Segovia stopped in mid-page, grabbed the guitar by the hole, brought it forward on his knee and just stared the audience down where the sound came from. It was a huge auditorium, and suddenly, you could hear a mouse pissing on cotton. Then he went back to playing. I remembered the incident well, and always behave myself at any performance since.

Just before this guy's starting to play, some attendants bring in a huge Plexiglas screen and put it between the guitarist and us. I had to wait till the end of the concert to find out what that was all about.

Seems the guy wouldn't play unless the screen was there. He'd heard that there could be assassins in the audience, and he wasn't about to get mistaken for Ray. Yeah, right, that reason and an age difference of about forty years and fifty pounds. He resembled Ray all right. Good thing the applause signs were there, cause we could hardly hear him. I did hear a lot of squeaks along the fret board though while the guy played. He mustn't be shopping at the same string store as Ray.

Ray used to do a lot of squeaking till he began to perfect both his technique, and someone put him on to strings made in Germany that were ground smooth on the bass side to reduce the effect of finger movement on the strings. Ray also used a silicone spray of some kind on his fingers too.

"Why didn't someone set up an amplifier?" I heard a fellow behind me ask. I'll bet a pro classical player would like to hear that one up close. Like in a dark alley. I was gonna explain, but I turn around, and Lula is giving me one of those stares that says hands off.

The guitar man played for twenty-five minutes, took a short break, came back and played for twenty more, then came back for one encore. I'm guessing that when they put this together, Ray'll do about the same. Ray used to give concerts that lasted about an hour. He finally worked up an hour program covered with two encore pieces.

We was all starved by the time it got done. They were supposed to feed us first, but I already explained that. There was a long table set up in the garden outside, while we were inside I presumed, since I hadn't noticed it when we walked by on the way in. There was these little things on what looked like crackers. Lula could've named all this stuff, but I wasn't about to ask her.

I'm looking around to see if Ray and Maartha are gonna show, but my nieces are distracting me, or so I figure. Ten minutes into food I see why. We look out at the helipad, a whirly bird starts to spin, and we see Ray and Maartha go out to chopper in a hurry. Ray does manage to wave toward our table just before he gets in. The blades are sending what's left of his hair all over the place. Then the chopper takes off and sends a dust devil our way on the trip out.

I look over at Rayette and Marthine, and a look of smug is on their pusses. "There's still some people they haven't found yet, who appear to be in Washington," Rayette says.

"You could've said something," Lula rebukes. "We're your relatives you know." She's not quite mad yet, but the girls don't want to see her when she is. She's already said it, so I don't bother. I simply ask if their folks are coming back soon, where they're headed and a few extras I make up for effect.

Nothing comes back. I look at Lula and she gives me one of those *I told you so* glances for about three seconds. We both know what's next. The girls have outgrown us. Will they ever be back to normal again? Does this experience do to them like it does to all the other inhabitants of the White House? Only the future can answer.

In about ten polite minutes, Lula and I are making our farewells to the girls and some of the guests. We'd like our limo driver real soon. They're real accommodating. Lula goes back in to get her wrap while I say goodbye to the girls. They're glad we came and are sorry once again that they missed us at our friend's place.

On the way back, I ask the driver to stop so I can get some Tums. He phones us back, and says to open a compartment on my lower right behind the seat in front of us. When I do, Walgreen's falls out all over the floor. There's stuff here that some drug stores back home never saw. I wade through several labels and find what I'm looking for, individually packaged. I take two, and stick two more in my pocket. Bob Schieffer'll be reporting this on his news show, part of a "It's Your Money" program. Hope he don't name me.

When we get to the hotel, Lula walks me to the front desk, and tells the clerk that we'll be checking out. She'd like our car brought out front in thirty minutes. She's boiling when she's like this. It's best if I just go along. Her teacher act is showing real good. Nobody better confront her before we get to the room.

Five in the evening heads us out of Washington, jammed in about the same amount of traffic as when we came in. All the folks who live here are coming home from a weekend away into the Blue Ridge. The Beltway'll be like this till midnight, I suppose. "Want me to drive?" I ask.

"No." she says, "Better nap."

I know what this means. She's gonna be full awake till about two in the morning. By then, it'll be too late to stop and get a motel. So we'll drive all night and get to our friends in time to wake them for breakfast. She calls them on the cell phone at about ten p.m. and warns them. They tell us where to meet them.

Fortunately, they're the kind of folks who are most accommodating and don't seem to mind whenever we come or what time it is. I sometimes wonder if this is really them, or they're acting this way because of our connections. I pick the first thought, however, when I consider how the second one has never showed itself. At least I don't think it has.

CHAP 35. Back toward the fort

We go out to breakfast at one of the restaurants that we've been to before with our exiled group in Columbia. Jack and Alma seem impressed that a waitress recognizes us all. She asks about how the *mission* went. Course she means our church sign on the side of the van.

Jack and Alma seem not to remember our church pretensions and instead are suddenly curious about what Lula and me been up to, and want a further explanation. Just what *mission* were *we* up to while in Washington? And how does this waitress know about it? The waitress takes our order and disappears.

We drop the waitress's reference. Lula and me begin to explain how we got put up miles away from Ray and family, and never did actually see him perform. Jack and Alma think the story's funny.

When the waitress brings our meal, she asks about one of the agents who was with us. "Do you think he'll call again?" she asks Lula.

Again? We never did see him get her phone number. But that's the FBI, or CIA or whoever they did represent, I forget.

But Alma pipes up to the waitress saying, "Oh sure, honey you can bet on it, darlin'. The Lord has been a watchin' over him since early day."

The rest of us is tryin' to keep a straight face. The little gal smiles while putting our orders on the table.

I can hardly move my elbows out of the way. I'm starting to get sleepy but Lula's full awake after three coffees, so I let her do all the talking.

"How was the concert?" Alma asks.

"Never did talk with or hear him," Lula says. Alma waits. "Oh we attended a concert, all right. Some other guitar player took the president's place. They're going to have my brother-in-law do his thing later, and then the whole scene is going to be blended by television techniques to come up with the total program. I suppose it'll be like everything was real, but it'll be virtual; in keeping with everything that's going on with computers right now, I suppose."

"How're they gonna manage that?" Jack asks. I don't even want to join in. Only Lula seems to understand.

"Well, what they do, if my niece told me correctly, is tape the audience. Then they'll tape the president playing at a later date. Then video editors will cut and paste sections to put them together, reconstructing the concert to show it taped simultaneously with the president doing the playing. That's all I can explain about it."

We still give Lula blank stares, though some of it starts to come through. I'm still braggin' on how it takes me two hours to get the clock on the VCR reset after a lightning storm. In Florida, I've been getting lots of practice.

"So this entire trip has been almost a waste. We got to see the president for about thirty seconds while he and Maartha boarded a helicopter on the White House lawn," Lula continues.

"Well, I still like your new dress," Alma adds. "Did your nieces like it?"

"You know, they never did comment about it. They seemed too preoccupied. They're into the pages and interns these days, aren't they Ray?"

"Hmmph?" I say, half asleep in the conversation.

"Better get you back," Jack says. "You can sleep all day. We'll wake you for supper."

"I'm fine," I shake my head, "but the sleep will be welcome. Got the check?" I ask Lula.

"Jack's already got it," she says.

I protest mildly.

***

During the day, while Lula and me are napping, the news reports tell about capturing some guys outside the on the White House lawn. Seems they were able to fake a landing posing like the official helicopter, then planned to storm the White House in a suicide mission. They got word that the president is home, and ready to go on with his concert, not knowing that Ray is still at Camp David. Are they surprised!

A bunch of vets visiting the Vietnam Memorial and touring the White house, assembled themselves and took on the intruders, capturing their weapons and turning them on the enemy. They then went over and blew up the helicopter. It all took place in a matter of about a half hour. One ex-soldier on our side was killed and two wounded. Six foreigners were killed in the attempt. They think they got them all.

Lula and me have slept through it all. Jack and Alma didn't want to wake us. It was probably better that way, since the edited reruns and daily assessments will be more interesting than first-hand.

By the time we get up for cocktails in late afternoon, Ray is back in the White House, and business is trying to restore itself.

All evening long we can't get anything but what's happened all day on television. Alma's missed her soaps. Jack's missed his Monday night fights. There was a special on

PBS that Lula was going to watch, but it's okay; she's still four books behind in her carry bag.

Jack and me are tired; me from not enough sleep and Jack from boredom. So we decide to take the boat out on the lake for a moonlight run to one of the clubs on the far shore. I'll bet no one is watching these events there.

On the way over, Jack's telling me how he managed to take all the rental gear that had been left in the boat back to the shop. He says they gave him a refund of almost half, for bringing it back early. He says he'd forward it to the government who rented it in the first place. Sure you will, Jack.

Seems the locals finally got wind of what was happening out on the lake. Someone, a friend of the rental shop owner, had been watching the proceedings of the diving on the lake with binoculars and had reported it back to the shop. When the shop owner got word, he began to circulate rumors about the diving going on to retrieve the downed bombers.

Word of mouth spread throughout town and by afternoon, he was inundated with people trying to rent gear. He'd had to refuse most and put some on a waiting list. So he was real glad to get his gear back when Jack brought it in. The generous refund would be more than ample in exchange for the prices for new rentals he told Jack. The owner said he was making calls to his franchise supplier to get more gear in by the end of the week. If we wanted some by then, he would give Jack a special discount.

Jack went on to tell me about the rumors that had been passed on about the diving people. Seems the binocular gal also mentioned that one of the divers looked very much like the First Lady. Nah, that was just rumor.

CHAP 36. A resolution

In the next few days after we get home, the story of the country's close call begins to unravel. At least, that's the version that is either true or someone has re-created it with embellishments. I like that word too.

One thing that the news anchors are trying to sort, with more than adequate help from experts, is how the Security Council got wind of the submarine and its efforts.

It seems there was an agent aboard, some Hebrew scholar, serving in communications officer capacity. He had been recruited in Latvia where he was on assignment trying to probe espionage records from World War Two survivors. There weren't many left. His actual work back in Israel had something to do with reconstructing Bible codes. There was some kind of book that came out not too long ago; it shed light on all kinds of stuff that already happened, that had been predicted. Some things to come, too. Lately there's been a lot of controversy about some of the literal translations of the Bible, as I get it. That's what I've been hearing of it all anyway. But back to the agent.

Somehow, this agent had infiltrated the Russian navy at one time and had some tours on submarines. Being an encryption expert and from Latvia, he had no problem getting into the Russian navy. Now, both the Russians and supposedly us too, are looking to find him. Some pundits think he went down with the sub, him being one of the last to be allowed to leave, according to some versions.

About two weeks later, the version about the submarine commander comes on the television. The FBI has been watching his house up in Idaho, and he never has returned. He's an American, and a former submarine commander; they've got it all figured by now. Don't ask me how they get that information. They always use the term, *from reliable sources*. They're pretty sure by now that if he didn't go down with the sub, he's either in Cuba or Russia. They get into his background on all the talk shows and on the fourteen news channels that we now have contributing to part of our monthly cable bill.

He's a disgruntled ex-military and submarine officer, who's had a string of personal problems, stretching way back to his being a maverick right from the start. Reminds me of some of the little ol' doggies Ray and me used to round up. Some you could never seem to keep in the herd.

When the guy did get into submarine service, first thing he wanted to do is pursue Russian subs and help turn Crazy Ivan's back on themselves. I don't presume to know the technicalities of all that. He had a death wish, so the pundits say.

When some of his crew started to protest, he began to make false reports about homosexual activities on the protestors. Says he could produce witnesses and got a few of them reassigned and discharged on his word. A commander was powerful in them days. Probably still are. The final coup though, was when some of his subordinates turned the wagon on him. He was finally brought up on sexual harassment charges himself. They found out later that these charges were probably made up. After he got into some trouble with women.

The charges was that he got lonely on some of those long undersea trips and made advances to some of the working crew. That's funny though when we heard how he got into trouble with one of his ranking officer's girls. Maybe he was bi. That's what the reports are saying anyhow. Anyway, he was gonna get court-martialed when some evidence turned up against him, and they gave him the option to resign.

From there, it was Idaho, and what has happened to him since. Just wanted to get even, they're saying. Think of it; one of our own trying to blow us up. Don't have to think too far though, with all that McVey stuff in Oklahoma a few years back. Well maybe not all of us, but what this government represents. Too bad they can't just pick out the bad apples.

I'm really worried about Ray in all of this. Maartha's kinda got her own agenda. But what has happened to Ray since he took office is getting beyond me. Why, when he was governor, he took no more guff off of folks than he'd yield to a canyon snake looking for water. If you'd a crossed him wrong, he'd be on you like a beaver on willow. That's the reason he got elected on a Independent ticket.

That's why I can't see him running from a confrontation, like taking that chopper when guests were waiting for him. Heck we could do without the concert, just so's we could have a chat. Seems ever since he got into the presidency, however, he's been doing other people's ideas, just saying a yes or no and going along. Maybe that's what that big office does to you. I ain't spoke to him about it yet, but I aim to.

CHAP 37. Added intrigue

About a month's gone by, and a lot more stuff has unraveled about the attempted coup, they're calling it. Not a coup really. After all, that commander didn't exactly recruit some of his buddies back home to overthrow the government.

Just a warning from Iran. That if they wanted to, they could get to us anytime. Like we didn't know that already with the recent scare.

Homeland Security— what a laugh. Course the guys on "Face The Nation" call it something else. Each one saying something different.

They've found out that the communications officer, you know, the Hebrew, relayed a code on a daily basis back to New York and to Iran, both. He encrypted it using Hebrew script from the Bible, in which sequences of letters, separated by uniform intervals were selected and transmitted. Did I just say all that? When reassembled, the letters spelled words that could be interpreted as instructions.

Once more, Commander Lasting, his name has been publicized now, authorized the use of ordinary e-mail to transmit the messages. What the commander didn't know, however, was that the New York contact was also one of ours. At the last minute, before the sub was going to launch missiles, the code had special salutations, already agreed upon, to let us know what was about to happen. That's when we deployed the sub chasers that would've actually had to wait until a first missile was fired before destroying the sub. There's some kind of agreement that we have about this. Seems stupid to me. If there's a hostile sub off our shores, and we don't know what it's doing there, just blow the bastard up. Ray would a done this while he was governor. *Execute them suckers*, he would a said.

In the coming days, they're gonna go down into the deep and try to find out what happened. They're also saying that they've got to hurry on this one, cause when they did that before, sometime back in the middle eighties when another sub had a accident and went down near the same place, they found someone

had already been there. When we tried to get
the missiles, the hatches were already opened
and no missiles were to be found. So Washington is saying now, it's up to us to salvage it
pronto, before any other recovery unit can do it.
Be just our luck, they say, to have those nuclear
warheads deteriorate and pour their contents
into the Gulf Stream, ending up on the Long Island seashore. Competition on the beaches with
hypodermic syringes and the like. Another excuse for staying out of the sun on weekends.

CHAP 38. Final resolution

Six months have gone by now, and Ray has called me twice, and I've done the same. We still haven't seen one another in person. We're planning a reunion, back home on the Salmon River, where we used to go to fish and camp. We've still got a cabin nearby where pops used to take us when we was kids. We're gonna put in a well, and Ray says he's thinking of putting in a few cattle and some fencing, after he gets out of office.

He's decided not to run a second term. Leftovers from the previous administration have left the economy in good shape, but are now starting to wear thin. Interest rates been steadily climbing. By the time he finishes office, he expects the economy'll be starting on a downward incline. He don't want to be part of that. The nation is always blaming the wrong guy for what happens to the economy, when what happens started years before, so he tells me.

"So what happened with the sub stuff?" I ask him on one of his calls.

"We got there in time. When we extracted one of the missiles, we found it had conventional warheads. They weren't planning to nuke us evidently. We just let the rest of them lay on the bottom."

"What about the crew?"

"Seems that Lasting released a few of them every so many hours just before the intended missile launch. That was what was so confusing to our side. We didn't know if he was turning to continue on his original mission to the coast of Iran or what. When he finally did settle, he had only a working crew aboard. The rest had been picked up, we think by Cubans, and are probably still on the beaches in Havana."

"Why'd he do it?"

"The same reasons you've heard about already on the news. He was trying to get even with the government, like that McVey guy who blew up the building in Oklahoma City."

"So, how's Maartha's exercise videos coming?" I say.

I tell him I bet Jack and Alma are getting a kick of watching her routine with the car spring his wife procured while she was at their house.

"Do they get a commission?" I ask.

"Ha-ha. She's doing fine. I almost never see her anymore. She's already planning to go international with some of her routines. The effect on the country has been great, don't you think? Already, we've got some statistical reports that the nation's youth have reduced their weights thorough exercise alone by point two five percent."

"Is that good?" I ask.

"She thinks it is, but keeps saying that's the same as twenty-five percent. I haven't got the inclination right now to set her straight. Mine has gone up by about twenty-five percent. All those dinner invites we get when we're campaigning."

"I thought you wasn't running again." I say.

"I'm not. But I still have to promote my successor."

"Oh, right. So you think we'll get together in the fall, then?"

"You bet. I can't wait. The girls'll be graduated and should be with us too. Rayette's going on to graduate school, and Marthine is joining her mother on an exercise tour of Australia. They're trying to get the wives of the beer drinkers on a program."

***

Not all of the submarine crew made it to Cuba. One member who escaped using an in-

flated raft was picked up by one of the aircraft
sent to locate the sub.

While aboard the raft, he continually sent
wireless signals about his location and was
eventually found and taken to Bermuda. There,
he was identified, debriefed and sent back to
Latvia for a new assignment. Among items he
withheld from investigators, however, were
files on his handheld: duplicates from files that
Commander Lasting had made, concerning
Swiss account information. On his way home,
he deplaned at a touchdown in Spain, where he
took a rental car to Switzerland for a vacation.

***

One Sunday evening, my neighbor, another Ed, bangs on our door. I answer. My
neighbor, panting says, "Are you watching it?
It's on PBS."

"What?" I say, trying to hide my beer behind my back that I've carried with me from the
sofa.

"You're on TV. You—and your brother
playing."

I invite him in.

There's Ray playing his concert, and once
in a while the camera drifts to the audience, and
there I am with Lula and the girls, all of us listening intently with sweet pusses on. When the
piece ends, we applaud, and in the diminishing
of the sound of our clapping, the announcer
says, "You are watching and listening to a live
performance from the . . ."

END

Notes:
Hybrid phrases in Gullah-speak created with use of a Gullah dictionary, <u>Gulluh For Oonuh/Gullah For You</u> by Virginia Mixson Geraty. 1998. Sandlapper Pub. Co.

CPSIA information can be obtained
at www.ICGtesting.com
Printed in the USA
LVHW100800150222
711153LV00003B/9

9 780615 188820